The Response of Higher Education Institutions to Regional Needs

ORGANISATION FOR ECONOMIC CO-OPERATION AND DEVELOPMENT

ORGANISATION FOR ECONOMIC CO-OPERATION AND DEVELOPMENT

Pursuant to Article 1 of the Convention signed in Paris on 14th December 1960, and which came into force on 30th September 1961, the Organisation for Economic Co-operation and Development (OECD) shall promote policies designed:

- to achieve the highest sustainable economic growth and employment and a rising standard of living in Member countries, while maintaining financial stability, and thus to contribute to the development of the world economy;
- to contribute to sound economic expansion in Member as well as non-member countries in the process of economic development; and
- to contribute to the expansion of world trade on a multilateral, non-discriminatory basis in accordance with international obligations.

The original Member countries of the OECD are Austria, Belgium, Canada, Denmark, France, Germany, Greece, Iceland, Ireland, Italy, Luxembourg, the Netherlands, Norway, Portugal, Spain, Sweden, Switzerland, Turkey, the United Kingdom and the United States. The following countries became Members subsequently through accession at the dates indicated hereafter: Japan (28th April 1964), Finland (28th January 1969), Australia (7th June 1971), New Zealand (29th May 1973), Mexico (18th May 1994), the Czech Republic (21st December 1995), Hungary (7th May 1996), Poland (22nd November 1996) and Korea (12th December 1996). The Commission of the European Communities takes part in the work of the OECD (Article 13 of the OECD Convention).

The Programme on Institutional Management in Higher Education (IMHE) started in 1969 as an activity of the OECD's newly established Centre for Educational Research and Innovation (CERI). In November 1972, the OECD Council decided that the Programme would operate as an independent decentralised project and authorised the Secretary-General to administer it. Responsibility for its supervision was assigned to a Directing Group of representatives of governments and institutions participating in the Programme. Since 1972, the Council has periodically extended this arrangement; the latest renewal now expires on 31st December 2001.

The main objectives of the Programme are as follows:

- to promote, through research, training and information exchange, greater professionalism in the management of institutions of higher education; and
- to facilitate a wider dissemination of practical management methods and approaches.

*
* *

Publié en français sous le titre :
LES ÉTABLISSEMENTS D'ENSEIGNEMENT SUPÉRIEUR FACE AUX BESOINS RÉGIONAUX

Foreword

This book aims to provide guidance to higher education managers to respond to a new set of actors and agencies, those concerned with regional development. It also sets out the formulation of policy by national and regional governments wishing to mobilise higher education institutions (HEIs) towards the achievement of regional development goals.

The report draws upon insights and case study material presented at conferences organised by the OECD programme on Institutional Management on Higher Education (IMHE) and which focused upon developments within the Baltic States and Scandinavia (held in Klaipeda, Lithuania); the United States (Fort Lauderdale, Florida); the United Kingdom (Edinburgh, Scotland); Australia (Byron Bay, New South Wales); and, continental Europe (Lyon, France). The case studies included a wide range of institutions from long established research-based universities striving to adjust traditional structures to new demands through to new institutions created with a specific commitment to meet regional needs. Therefore, the report is not just about regional universities established with a highly focused mission.

In addition to institutional diversity the case studies also embrace a wide range of regional conditions under which HEIs are operating, particularly in terms of local prosperity and economic performance. No attempt has been made to classify these contexts since the report is concerned with the response of HEIs to regional needs whatever these might be; it is not primarily about the role of universities in reducing regional disparities (although this can be an important role for universities in terms of public policy).

A further source of diversity for the case studies is the context provided by national higher education policy. Accordingly, the case study material is supplemented by other sources of information about national higher education policy, including major national surveys of higher education in the United Kingdom, Australia and Finland each of which embrace the regional agenda. These sources reveal great variation between countries in: the autonomy and financial resources available to HEIs to respond to regional needs; the extent of national planning or regulation of higher education at a sub-national level including the relationship between different levels of the education system (polytechnics, universities, further education colleges); and, the scope for regional agencies to directly fund universities.

OECD 1999

The material in the report is presented in terms of key questions, or points of inquiry, which are likely to confront those concerned with mobilising HEI resources, either as university managers, agencies directly responsible for regional development, or national policy makers with responsibility for higher education and for territorial development. Where appropriate, the text is supported by examples of good practice within institutions in managing the institution/regional interface or in the implementation of national/regional policy.

This book is published on the responsibility of the Secretary-General of the OECD.

Acknowledgements

This report has been prepared under the guidance of Professor John Goddard, Pro Vice-Chancellor and Professor of Regional Development Studies at the University of Newcastle upon Tyne, the United Kingdom, who headed the IMHE project on the response of higher education institutions. The report was drafted by Dr Paul Chatterton, Research Associate at the Centre for Urban and Regional Development Studies at the University of Newcastle upon Tyne.

The conferences were organised by the IMHE secretariat, notably Kari Hyppönen and Pierre Laderrière and the local organisers were Stasys Vaitekûnas (Klaipeda), Mantha Mehallis (Florida), Martin Lowe (Edinburgh), Zbys Klich (Byron Bay), and Pierre Laderrière (Lyon).

Additional material on the national higher education policy context was provided by Professor Zbys Klich (Australia), Jean-Paul de Gaudemar and Jan Karlsson (France), Kari Hyppönen (Finland), and Francesc Solé Parellada and Josep Coll (Spain).

Special thanks are due to Peter West, Secretary at the University of Strathclyde, the United Kingdom, who acted as Chair of the Project Steering Committee and to Professor Zbys Klich, Pro Vice-Chancellor of Southern Cross University, Australia, for his assistance to Professor Goddard and Dr Chatterton in the preparation of the final report.

Table of Contents

OECD 1999

1

Introduction

Context

The autonomous teaching and research activities of publicly funded universities are coming under increasing pressure from governments and their electorates. The agenda has moved on from a desire to simply increase the general education level of the population and the output of scientific research; there is now a greater concern to harness university education and research to specific economic and social objectives. Nowhere is this demand for specificity more clear than in the field of regional development. While universities are located in regions, questions are being asked about what contribution they make to the development of those regions. Whilst it might be possible to identify passive impacts of universities in terms of direct and indirect employment, how can the resources of universities be mobilised to actively contribute to the development process? Such questions are being posed because development has a strong territorial dimension – national objectives can only be achieved by realising the full potential of constituent sub-national units and in this regard universities in different regions are being required to make a contribution. So the challenge universities face is how should they respond to demands which are emanating from a set of actors and agencies which have hitherto not sought to engage in a dialogue with universities, namely those concerned with regional development.

This perspective on development reflects new industrial dynamics, processes which are well captured by the couplet "globalisation and localisation". Thus, it is the nature of the local environment for the production of goods and services which is as important as the national macro-economic situation in determining the ability of businesses to remain competitive within global markets. Within the local environment, the availability of knowledge and skills is as relevant as the physical infrastructure and in this regard, the regionally engaged university becomes a key locational asset and a powerhouse for economic development.

Characteristically, such environments are places with dynamic connections between the enhancement of skills, processes of industrial and service innovation, and the wider cultural development agenda which can be referred to as a "learning region". Alongside these economic drivers are political pressures for decentralisation of power to regions, not least to enable them to have the autonomy

OECD 1999

to create locally tailored operating environments for economic success within the global economy. Again, universities are being asked to make a contribution to this regional institutional capacity building.

It could be argued that universities have always made a wider contribution to the economy and society in the places which they are located – for example, through non-vocational education, research support for local firms, public lectures, concerts and access to museums and galleries. What is emerging now is a demand to recognise this activity as a "third role" for universities not only sitting alongside, but integrated with, mainstream teaching and research.

Responding to these regionally specific demands clearly requires new kinds of resources and new forms of leadership and management in higher education that enable universities to become a dynamic problem solving think-tank for, and supplier of, knowledge and skills required by the regional clients they serve. As such, regional engagement embraces many of the facets of the "responsive university" being generated by part of the wider agenda within higher education.

In the past, higher education in most countries was primarily funded by national governments to meet national labour market needs for skilled manpower and to provide a capacity to meet national research and technological development needs. In terms of higher education management this has generally meant a single paymaster, relatively secure long-term funding, the education of a readily identifiable and predictable population of full-time students in the 18-24 year age range and destined to work in the corporate sector and the provision of a well-founded infrastructure to support the pursuit of individual academic research and scholarship. Such a regime imposes limited demands on university management and indeed supports the ethos of academic self-management and collegiality.

This world is being replaced by a number of new realities many of which have a strong regional dimension. These include the move from a system of elite to mass higher education; meeting the needs of a larger and more diverse client population; lifelong learning needs created by changing patterns of skills demands in the labour market; declining public support for students which in some countries leads to more attending their local university; increased competition from providers of education on a global scale; new ways of delivering education and training made possible by information and communication technologies (ICTs) and, last but not least, the changing nature of knowledge production and distribution which is challenging the monopolistic position of universities. For many universities, regional engagement is therefore becoming the crucible within which an appropriate response to many of the challenges raised by these overall trends within higher education policy is being forged.

Figure 1 attempts to summarise the above discussion in diagrammatic form. It focuses upon the processes which link together all of the components within the university and the region into a learning system. Within the university, the challenge is to link the teaching, research and community service roles by internal mechanisms (funding, staff development, incentives and rewards, communications,

Figure 1. **University/region value added mechanisms**

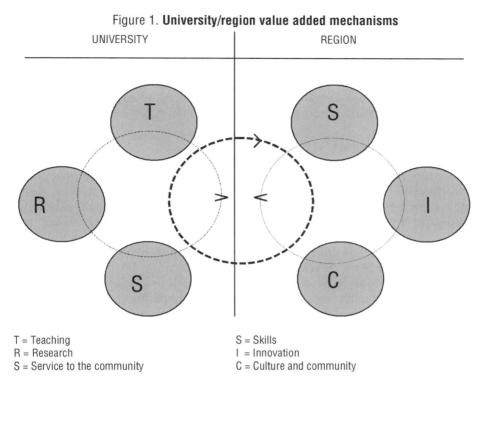

UNIVERSITY   REGION

T = Teaching   S = Skills
R = Research   I = Innovation
S = Service to the community   C = Culture and community

.... Value added university management processes

.... Value added regional management processes

▬ ▬ ▬ ▬. University/regional dynamic interface

Source: Goddard and Chatterton (1999).

etc.) which make these activities more responsive to regional needs. These linkages represent "value added management processes". Within the region, the challenge for universities is to engage in many of the facets of the development process (such as skills enhancement, technological development and innovation and cultural awareness) and link them with the intra university mechanisms in a "university/region value added management process". Put another way, the successful university will be a learning organisation in which the whole is more than the sum of its parts and the successful region will have similar dynamics in which the university is a key player. This challenge has been neatly summarised by Duke (1998, p. 5):

> "For universities, the learning region may be the best kept secret of the dying days of this century. In practical terms this implies blending and

combining competition in the new enterprise environment with collaboration; fostering and supporting boundary spanners who can work across the borders of the university in effective discourse with other organisations and their different cultures; fostering cultural change to enable universities to speak and work with partners from many traditions and persuasions as more learning organisations emerge and together enrich their various overlapping learning zones or regions."

Approach to the report

This report is based upon an on-going project within the OECD's programme on Institutional Management in Higher Education (IMHE). The primary objective of this project is to provide guidance to higher education managers seeking to respond to a new set of actors and agencies, those concerned with regional development. The secondary objective is to guide the formulation of policy by national and regional governments seeking to mobilise HEIs towards the achievement of regional development goals.

The umbrella term "HEI" is used in recognition of the variety of institutional forms in terms of history, size, market position and funding sources covered by the report. More importantly, the term HEI reflects a growing blurring of the boundary between institutions undertaking research and awarding higher degrees (universities) and those undertaking sub-degree work and further and vocational education. Thus, as part of their growing regional role, many universities undertake sub-degree teaching and offer postgraduate diplomas whilst some community or further education colleges award degrees validated by universities within their region or elsewhere. Although managing the boundary between universities and other institutions is becoming a regional higher education policy issue, the contributions to this report focus on the university sector.

The report falls into three parts. The first part (Chapters 2-4) expands upon the discussion of regional development processes and higher education policy. It highlights trends at three scales – international, national and regional – which are influencing management across all HEIs. The discussion explores the interrelationships between levels for many HEIs. For example, most older universities are global institutions in terms of their research and student recruitment and have been involved in "nation-building" but are now facing demands for local engagement as a result of new economic and political drivers. Following a largely theoretical discussion on HEIs and territories in Chapter 2, Chapter 3 provides evidence about how these universal dynamics are being worked out in the context of different national higher education policy environments with detailed national reviews covering the United Kingdom, Australia, the United States, Spain, France and Finland being provided in Appendix 2. The nature of the regional context is discussed in Chapter 4 in terms of the influence of regional interest groups (or stakeholders) on the development of higher education institutions via governance, funding and planning mechanisms. Particular attention is paid to the role of the European Union which has specifically engaged with the universities and regions agenda within member states as part of its regional policy and in so doing has connected the three geographical scales covered in the report.

The second part of the report (Chapters 5-8) discusses the response of HEIs to the changing context mapped out in Chapters 2-4. Chapter 5 provides an overview of the mechanisms for regional engagement being adopted by HEIs both in terms of internal and boundary spanning processes. Chapters 6, 7 and 8 focus upon specific management processes in the three roles of teaching, research and community service.

The third part (Chapters 9 and 10) provides the conclusions and recommendations with the former summarising the factors driving the adoption of a regional role by HEIs and the barriers that might be inhibiting progress on this front. Finally, the recommendations are targeted at those actors and agencies which have the resources and responsibilities to enhance regional engagement or eliminate barriers.

Throughout the report, recommendations emphasise *processes* of institutional management and regional development. Because of the diversity of national and regional contexts and of individual institutional profiles, no attempt is made to prescribe what specific priorities should be identified by HEIs and regions. What programmes should be pursued to maximise benefits both to the institution and the region is something that has to be worked out on a case by case basis. The objective of this report is to aid the development of a common understanding of the issues involved on the part of all the stakeholders and not to produce a universally applicable methodology for identifying which initiatives will bring the greatest rewards to either HEIs or their regions.

2

Higher Education Institutions and Territoriality

The capacity of an HEI to respond to regional needs is influenced by conditions which result from the inter-relations between several geographic scales from the global to the local and also from the historical legacy of each HEI and its region. Policy makers need to be aware of the demands exerted upon HEIs from each of these different spatial scales. These include: restructuring in the global economy; changing national contexts for higher education; the particular characteristics of the region in terms of the regional economic base; regional policy; the regional educational system and the particularities of each institution. This chapter discusses this context for HEIs through a review of territoriality and HEIs.

Problematising territoriality

- ♦ What would the HEI define as its territorial remit?
- ♦ What management structures should be in place within HEIs to manage the portfolio of different territorial roles?
- ♦ How can HEIs expand national and international activity whilst still meeting regional needs?
- ♦ Do mechanisms exist to embed a belief that the institution can, and should, operate within different territorial levels for the benefit of the region?

Territoriality is an extremely complex and problematic concept for HEIs. Universities, in particular, exist as autonomous institutions which are often characterised by low levels of local territorial embeddedness, regulation at the national level and preoccupation with international and national academic and research communities. All HEIs embrace some notion of territoriality within their mission statements and institutional plans; these range from general notions of contributing to "society" and international research to more precise commitments to local and regional communities. A report for the Association of European

Universities stressed the growing urgency for HEIs to take engagement with external partners seriously:

"In order to respond better to the needs of different groups within society, universities must engage in a meaningful dialogue with stakeholders ... universities which do not commit themselves to open and mutually beneficial collaboration with other economic, social and cultural partners will find themselves academically as well as economically marginalised." (Davies, 1998)

Moreover, the UNESCO's *Framework for Priority Action for Change and Development of Higher Education"* (1998) has stated that governments and policy makers should:

"Develop innovative schemes of collaboration between institutions of higher education and different sectors of society to ensure that higher education and research programmes effectively contribute to local, regional and national development."

In spite of these positive statements, the issue of how they should respond to regional needs is relatively uncharted territory for most HEIs, especially for the older and more comprehensive universities. Most HEIs strive towards teaching and research activity of national and international significance. Thus a recent survey of the United Kingdom universities asked senior managers to comment on how they could best describe the territorial role of their institution. Only 2% described their university as "a community-based institution serving the needs of the local area/region", whilst nearly half described it as "an institution seeking to contribute to the local area and also develop international strengths" and one-third described it as "an international research institution seeking to provide support to the local community where it does not conflict with international research excellence" (DfEE, 1998a).

Research within HEIs tends towards an international/national rather than a regional perspective and this reflects the priorities of governments and their research councils as the main funders of research. Clearly, research with a regional perspective can increase as the funding base of HEIs is diversified, but most universities are reluctant to increase regionally-based teaching or research as they see this as the role of the non-university higher education sector. Moreover, it is often the opinion of regional partners that the best way for HEIs to meet regional needs is by functioning as a national and international centre of teaching and research excellence.

The institutional profile (such as funding sources, balance between teaching and research, size, etc.) of an HEI is an important determinant on its territorial focus. However, the connections between institutional profile and territoriality are extremely complex. For example, HEIs that are highly specialised as training or technical institutions, may either be local or globally orientated institutions. Moreover, large comprehensive universities whilst developing strong international and national teaching and research activities also have the resource base to engage with the region.

The issue of territoriality also raises the issue of ownership. HEIs which operate within nationally regulated and funded regimes generally function as autonomous institutions and have control over the nature of teaching and research. However, the introduction of a regional agenda within such national systems requires a stronger regional planning framework which brings together a number of regional stakeholders to co-manage and co-ordinate and regulate the management and funding of teaching and research. Such mechanisms may challenge that autonomy.

HEIs, then, operate within multiple and overlapping territories and usually manage a portfolio of activities ranging from the global to the local. The advantage of the presence of one or more HEIs in a region, is that expertise from these different scales can be a major asset to the community. The challenge is to manage simultaneously the various territorial portfolios so that they reinforce each other and to establish mechanisms through which the national and international connections of HEIs can be mobilised to benefit the region.

Although many HEIs are adopting a rhetoric of regionalism within their mission statements, the term "region" can be equated by some academics with parochialism and be seen as the antithesis of being metropolitan and cosmopolitan – adjectives which are heavily associated with the historical development of many old universities. Moreover, the term "region" can refer to many different scales. It can refer to the immediate hinterland, a large part of a country, a state in federal countries or wider pan-national areas. In particular, regions are emerging, or are being defined, which cross national boundaries and consist of elements from several national territories. Thus there are pan-national regions such as the Baltic and Scandinavian regions, the Pacific region incorporating Australia and South-East Asia, and the European Community.

It is also important to appreciate the multiplicity of ways in which an explicitly regional role for an HEI can be interpreted. For example, a self-conscious regional HEI may be defined by associating itself legally or through its name with a particular territory; by operating within a regional recruitment area; by interacting with regional research partners and the regional industrial base; or by offering service and outreach facilities to the regional community. HEIs, then, have many justifications for calling themselves "regional" institutions according to the way in which the relationship with the region, and its stakeholders, is prioritised.

It is clear, then, that the issue of territoriality for HEIs is problematic. It is vital for all those who work in, or come into contact with, HEIs to appreciate these issues of territoriality and the ways in which they are addressed within HEIs compared to most other public and private institutions.

Reconceptualising territorial development and governance

The changing role of HEIs in regional development must be seen within a broader context of globalisation and the changing nature of regional development and governance, notably the shift in emphasis from material to non-material assets (knowledge, skills, culture, institutions) and the resurgence of the region as an important arena for political and economic activity. This section briefly reviews this changing context and outlines new forms of territorial governance based upon the concept of the learning region.

New forms of regional development

For effective regional engagement it is vital that those steering the regional interests of HEIs develop an understanding of the enormous transformations which have occurred in the capitalist world economy since the mid-1970s. This can be viewed in terms of a shift in phases of capitalist development from a system based upon mass production, Keynesianism, macro-economic management and the welfare state to one characterised by widespread economic and political de-regulation and the emergence of more decentralised forms of economic organisation. These changes have had major implications for economic development strategies and territorial governance especially in terms of the dynamics which have been brought to bear upon securing regional economic success from the twin processes of globalisation and localisation.

The post-war period until the mid-1970s represented a highly regulated economic and political regime in the west known as Fordism which was characterised by the mass production of standard goods, a strong state-led social welfare system and a strong division of labour tasks. However, it is posited that this system has now given way to an emerging regulatory system of post-Fordism characterised by a new, and more regional, geography of capitalist activity. A number of features can be discerned within this system, all of which have resonances for the management of HEIs.

Firstly, the economy itself is becoming more regionalised in that there is a new geography of capitalist activity associated with, on the one hand, the growing internationalisation of production and the mobility of global capital flows and, on the other, the declining regulatory capacity of the nation-state. This shift entails a resurgence of the region through the integration of production at a regional level and the decentralisation of large corporations into clusters of smaller business units and the greater role of smaller businesses as sub-contractors, suppliers and franchisees. Economic activity, then, is dominated by interfirm relationships and "collaborative manufacturing" which emerges at the regional level and allows both competition and collaboration to flourish. While nation-states remain the basic unit of economic and political organisation, they are losing their monopoly on policy making, representation, legitimacy and questions of identity.

In the wake of this declining regulatory capacity of the nation-state, the institutions which regulate economic activity are being regionalised. At a regional level, an array of intermediate organisations are emerging which create in any particular locality an "institutional thickness" (Amin and Thrift, 1994) comprised of a membership of institutions which will typically include firms, chambers of commerce, government agencies, R-D laboratories, training and educational institutions including universities. This membership constitutes the basis for co-operative or associative forms of governing localities which signify a shift from state regulation to regional self-regulation. Moreover, these networks rely upon animateurs who generate dialogue between the various organisations. The success of this network of organisations is underpinned by a "soft infrastructure" or what has been called "social capital" (Putnam et al., 1993) and "untraded interdependencies" (Storper, 1995), where economic success is dependent upon trust, norms, values and tacit and personal knowledge. These are key elements of the environment within which regional networks of interfirm organisation are established and grow.

Local and regional policy, then, has had to become innovative and entrepreneurial itself, typically through drawing on a wider network of resources, negotiating and building alliances between local and other tiers of government, universities, private sector interests and non-profit organisations. Thus the successful entrepreneurial municipality shifts from being an arm of the national welfare state to a catalyst for local co-operation and policy innovation. The importance of this perspective for managing firms and localities has been neatly captured by Kanter (1995) in her book *World Class* which is significantly subtitled "Thriving Locally in the Global Economy". According to Kanter:

"In the future, success will come to those companies, large and small, that can meet global standards and tap into global networks. And it will come to those cities, states and regions that do the best job of linking the businesses that operate within them to the global economy."

She argues that forces of globalisation are so powerful that communities must connect the global and the local and create a civic culture to attract and retain or "embed" footloose investment. The challenge is to find ways in which the global economy can work locally by unlocking those resources which distinguish one place from another. The essential argument here is that HEIs can provide a vital locational asset and competitive advantage for regions within the global economy.

Localities increasingly have to compete with other cities and regions around the world. Kanter (1995) calls this "the infrastructure for collaboration," where local communities have to adopt more self-reliant practices and a cosmopolitan and outward looking attitude to be successful in the global economy. Basically, communities have to adopt a number of strategies, such as co-operative alliances and leadership programmes to be able to compete in the global economy.

Geographical differences in the nature of cultures, institutions and legacies of past industrial practices will clearly influence the effectiveness of the dissemination of knowledge between and within institutions. For example, differences in training cultures and attitudes towards technology are also crucial to the effectiveness of modes of communication and exchange. What these shifts in the organisation of economic activity point to is the need for localities to embed global capital by fostering a civic culture and collective approaches to regional economic development. As Florida (1995) observed:

"The shift to knowledge-intensive capitalisation goes beyond the particular business and management strategies of individual firms. It involves the development of new inputs and a broader infrastructure at the regional level on which individual firms and production complexes can draw. The nature of this economic transformation makes regions key economic units in the global economy – the new age of capitalism has shifted the nexus of competition to ideas; regions must adopt the principles of knowledge creation and continuous learning; they must in effect become learning regions."

These changes, such as the globalisation of finance, and of the organisation of production, and the weakened bargaining power of the nation state, have been underpinned by the rate of technological change, most notably through the widespread effects of generic or carrier technologies such as information and communication technologies (ICTs). Technological innovation and access to resources for innovation (skills, knowledge, information) have become central to the competitive strategy of firms, which have developed new flexible structures to better utilise and capture such advantages on a global scale. States have recognised the need to maintain a position on the leading edge of technology if they are to maintain employment and growth, and hence there is an increasing attention to policies to support and promote R-D, innovation and technology transfer. International bodies have encouraged greater freedom in the flow of goods and information such that now it is the nature of the production locality as much as national market characteristics that determine investment decisions. Not only has regional or local intervention become more important to economic success, but there has also been a qualitative shift in the form of local policy towards indigenous entrepreneurship and innovation, and to providing a more sophisticated environment for mobile capital so as to maximise local value added (R-D and other high status jobs, successful and therefore growing firms).

The learning region

The most helpful approach to operationalising the role of HEIs in this new economic environment can be found in the concept of the learning economy which emerges from studies of national systems of innovation (Lundvall, 1992; Lundvall and Johnson, 1994). Lundvall defines the learning economy as an economy where the success of individuals, firms and regions, reflects the capability to learn (and forget old practices); where change is rapid and old skills get obsolete and new skills are in demand; where learning includes the building of competencies, not just increased access to information; where learning is going on in all parts of society, not just high-tech sectors; and where net job creation is in knowledge intensive sectors (high R-D, high proportion with a university degree, and job situation worsens for the unskilled). The learning region depends upon network knowledge which refers not only to the skills of individuals but the transfer of knowledge from one group to another to form learning systems – the institutional infrastructure of public and private partnerships. Because network knowledge is highly dependant on interpersonal relations, it can most readily be developed within a particular region.

Moreover, the link between the information society, ICTs and learning regions is considered to be mutual and self-reinforcing. Regions with strong learning cultures that support the development and uptake of ICT applications may be able to develop competitive advantages and utilise the information society as a mechanism for growth, whilst the ICTs themselves are constructed through certain social networking processes and contexts to be found in particular regions (the Silicon Valley phenomenon). For less favoured regions the implications are clear: without some attempt to make better use of ICTs the prospects of cohesion and convergence are poor.

So where do universities fit into this debate? Historically, universities have played a key role in nation building and continue to underpin a wide range of national institutions through the participation of academic staff in numerous public bodies. However, as the economy becomes more regionalised, universities, through their resource base of people and skills and knowledge increasingly play a significant role in regional networking and institutional capacity building. Staff, either in formal or informal capacities, can act as regional animateurs through representation on outside bodies ranging from school governing boards and local authorities to local cultural organisations and development agencies. Universities also act as intermediaries in the regional economy by providing, for example, commentary and analysis for the media. Universities, then, make an indirect contribution to the social and cultural basis of effective democratic governance, and ultimately, economic success through the activities of autonomous academics.

Moreover, in this more regionalised economy, universities are confronted by a new client base in terms of both teaching and research. Traditional relationships with large corporations and nationally-based firms and research organisations are being supplemented by a new regional client base comprised of clusters of firms and the emergence of regionally-based supply chains of small and medium enterprises (SMEs). Such trends have important implications for the skills required of graduates and the way in which universities manage the interface between degree courses and the labour market. It is therefore not surprising that regional agencies are promoting graduate retention initiatives as a way of upgrading the stock of higher level local skills.

In parallel with these demand side changes, the expansion of higher education provision together with rising numbers experiencing the need to change career later on in life is leading to a growing supply of mature local students for undergraduate and postgraduate programmes. In particular, there is a greater demand for the provision of vocational and professional education from universities which reflects the needs of the regional economy. Universities have much to gain in adapting to these evolving realities of a more regional economy. In particular, regional networking can be thought of as an institutional survival or strengthening strategy for universities in that the regional economy needs to offer opportunities so that the learning and teaching from within HEIs can be implemented externally. In this sense, a strong and supportive regional economy will create a competitive university, and a strong university has more to offer a region.

Finally, in the context of the lifelong learning agenda, learning and teaching activities have moved away from a linear model of transmission of knowledge based upon the classroom and are becoming more interactive and experiential, drawing upon, for example, project work and work-based learning much of which is location specific. Within this changed context, learning and knowledge creation take on different characteristics. In particular, it is important to differentiate between codifiable knowledge (know-what, such as data, etc.) and tacit knowledge such as know-how (skills), know-who (networking) and know-why (experience). These latter forms of "hybrid knowledge", then, become the most valuable type of knowledge depending upon interpersonal relationships, trust and co-operation and most readily developed within the region. Because interactive forms of learning are inherently bound in particular localities, university teaching and research shows tendencies towards localisation, or regionalisation. It is within this new regional context for learning and knowledge that connections can be forged between the teaching and research agendas of universities. In particular, the university acts as a conduit through which research of an international and national nature is transferred to specific localities through the teaching curriculum.

A key challenge within the learning region is to mobilise a wide group of regional stakeholders, including HEIs and their staff and students, to develop learning networks to enhance the wider political and cultural leadership of their localities. However, in the absence of direct funding streams for regional activity and in the context of nationally-driven and competitive systems for teaching and research funds and student recruitment, many HEIs play a limited role in developing learning networks at the regional level. It should be emphasised that universities, whatever their missions, remain autonomous institutions with allegiances to multiple territories rather than specific regions. In this regard, their relationship with territory is more ambivalent than that of public authorities with a legally defined domain.

One key area of concern is the use of ICTs to harness new forms of educational provision associated with the idea of the "virtual university" as an extension of the traditional place based institutions. Many view the coming of the information society as a threat to the university wherein the potential role of the university in a region is countered by its weakening setting for learning. In particular, access to the Internet for students may affect the status and authority of university teachers, undermining their knowledge monopoly. The emergence of electronic management of university education with the "hollowing out" of existing universities through on-line course provision by self-employed academics may therefore disembed learning from its regional setting. All such major developments will pose threats and opportunities for regions struggling to adapt to the needs of the learning economy, and policies for education, training, innovation, research and regional development all need to take into account how HE systems might be affected by such developments.

This new environment confronting universities from within higher education and from regions contains important implications for institutional management. In particular, it requires universities to act corporately and to respond to the demands of a new and diverse set of clients and agencies representing them, many of whom are directly or indirectly concerned with regional development. Such dynamics concerning global economic and political restructuring and the concomitant emergence of new forms of territorial governance based upon the "region" are a vital back-drop, then, for those steering HEIs in their efforts to formulated strategies to meet regional needs.

However, the extent to which the regional organisation of economic activity as set out above implies sustainable regional development is unclear, especially in the light of the dependency of many regional economies on footloose global inward investment and branch-plant activity. In this sense, there are trends towards a heightened differentiation of performance between core and peripheral regions as a result of a more open and unregulated global economic and political system. HEIs can play an important brokerage role within regions in terms of promoting debate on the suitability of different models of regional development and their ability to meet the needs of the regional population.

OECD 1999

3

Characteristics of the National Systems

Although this report concerns the response of HEIs to regional needs, it is important to appreciate the influence of the national policy context and the characteristics of the national HE system on the ability of HEIs to engage with their region. The governance of the regional development process is, in part, a negotiation between the region and the nation state; and many regional bodies receive substantial funding from central government and operate within some form of nationally regulated environment. In contrast, HEIs tend to operate within a national system, and major policy shifts affecting their orientation towards their locality are usually driven by national policy agendas. This section highlights the changing nature of HE policy at the national level and discusses some of the implications for institutional engagement with the regions.

National systems of higher education

- ♦ What are the dominant characteristics of the national higher education system – for example, binary, unified, comprehensive?
- ♦ What characterises inter-institutional relationships – co-operation, competition, market-led?
- ♦ To what extent is there dialogue between government ministries concerned with territorial development and those sponsoring higher education?

Many HEIs, especially the older universities, have played, and still play, a significant role in the process of nation-building and the formation of a national identity. For instance, universities such as Oxford and Cambridge in Britain and Harvard and Yale in the United States are central elements which communicate a sense of nationhood to the outside world. However, the extent to which HEIs continue to play a role within nation-state building is coming under increasing scrutiny as a result of the challenges outlined above.

Many differences exist in the national context within which HE has developed. For example, the older systems of HE in the continental European heartland of France, Germany and Italy represent largely unreformed and heavily *centrally* managed HE systems. In these national contexts, most HEIs are not subject to multiple pressures to engage with their regions. In contrast, Scandinavian and Anglo-American countries have recently displayed tendencies towards greater institutional self-management and regional engagement. However, even in those cases where regionalism has been introduced into the management of higher education, there are still aspects of central regulation.

Moreover, numerous types of national HE systems exist such as university-dominated, "binary", "unified" or "comprehensive". For example, Britain has a strong history of university-dominated higher education, a pattern which is repeated in several Mediterranean countries such as Spain, Greece, Italy and Portugal. Germany has recently introduced and expanded a binary system whilst Australia has recently abolished such a division. Moreover, in countries such as France non-university institutions enjoy more equal status even within a binary system.

However, what is evident is that in the light of mass higher education provision, national higher education systems are becoming more alike (Scott, 1995). In particular, dualism has been replaced by a unified system in Britain (1992), Australia (1988) and Sweden (1977). There is also a growing recognition of the need for comprehensive systems, where higher education is conceived as a total system and institutions are allocated specific roles within it. One of the most well developed examples of this is the Californian model in the United States.

What these examples highlight is that the specific characteristics of national higher education systems is a significant influence on the ability of HEIs to respond to growing external demands and to engage in regional development. Moreover, central government funding and management policies towards HEIs determine, in part, the freedom which individual institutions have to pursue regional agendas. Many HEIs function within a national system which grants them much institutional autonomy in terms of the orientation of teaching and research activities. In other contexts, the national agenda exerts a strong influence on the orientation of the institution. For example, in 1997 the Swedish Parliament amended the law governing higher education institutions and Swedish universities are now instructed to undertake – in addition to teaching and research – an additional role of "co-operation with the outside world and promotion and development of the society at large". This third role obliges universities to interact more closely with their environment.

The issue of the regional role of HEIs is being examined in several national policy contexts. In the 1960s, many governments used HEIs as tools of regional development to promote regional convergence between core and peripheral areas. More recently, there is a growing convergence between the concerns of agencies with responsibility for territorial development and those in charge of the management of higher education. Such concerns are associated with the need to mobilise a large group of stakeholders, including HEIs, to contribute to the regional development process and to create a strong sense of partnership and civic responsibility in the locality.

A number of national contexts demonstrate these concerns with territoriality. For example, in Britain the higher education sector has not been overly influenced by regional needs, but there has been evidence of recent moves towards a regional agenda within this sector through the Dearing Inquiry (1997) and subsequent policy shifts such as the establishment of regional advisors within the Higher Education Funding Council and the Regional Development Agencies on which some universities are represented. However, there has been some opposition from British universities in terms of the introduction of greater national planned system of HE at the regional level. France is also slowly moving away from a heavily centralised system of higher education whilst the United States have a well established and planned system of higher education within individual states. Finally, in Finland a number of HEIs were established as part of the government's policy of encouraging regional development in remote areas. (A fuller discussion of regional dimensions to higher education policy in Australia, Finland, France, Spain, the United Kingdom and the United States is provided in Appendix 1.)

Regional higher education systems in a national context

♦ To what extent does the financing and management of HEIs occur at a regional level?
♦ Are there regional organisations that have strategic responsibility over funding and management of HEIs?
♦ Is there any inter-regional collaboration on issues such as student recruitment, and the financing of teaching and research?

Many different types of systems of education can be discerned which are determined, in part, by the number and type of education partners, the range of co-operative activities and the existence of regulating or lead organisations. Four categories have been identified which characterise different types of higher education systems (Davies, 1997):

- *Overt competition* – in which regional business is limited and institutions compete for market share using strategies such as specialisation and pricing policies.
- *Regulation* – in which each HEI has a prescribed role demonstrated in HE systems such as in Germany and the United States.
- *Collaboration/horizontal integration* – in which co-operation stems from the institution as a response to external pressures rather than governmental mechanisms.
- *Vertical integration* – in which strategic partnerships are established to develop franchising and credit arrangements. Quasi-federations or full institutional mergers may result.

However, the extent to which decentralised and regional authorities contribute to the funding, management and planning (in terms of for example, student numbers, curriculum design, research activity and community service) of higher education varies greatly between OECD Member countries. For example in France, regional authorities on average fund a third of final expenditure on higher education, yet the variation around this average is great (de Gaudemar, 1997). There are two main models: the centralised model in which the national government is the main source of funds (for example, Finland, France, Hungary, Italy, Japan, New Zealand, the United Kingdom) and the decentralised model where the regional authorities are the main source of funds (for example, Australia, Canada, Germany, Spain, the United States).

The are few systematic moves, then, towards the emergence of coherent planned and funded systems of HE at the regional level and most higher education systems remain regulated at the national level in terms of student numbers, course content, funding and institutional management. However, in certain countries, subnational structures exist with specific remits for the management and funding of HEIs such as the German *Länder*, the Spanish autonomous communities and the federal states of the United States. The United States is a particularly good example of a well developed and regulated higher education systems at a subnational level which involves state defined roles and student quotas for individual institutions and state-wide management boards. However, the United States is an exception rather than the rule especially in terms of the localised nature of the funding base of HEIs derived from sources such as state taxation and regional alumni, and their commitment to the community through the land grant tradition.

In the case of Germany, complete control over all aspects of education rests with the 16 states rather than the federal government. In this sense, financial and administrative responsibility for HEIs rests with each individual state, in the state capital, rather than the national government. In spite of this regional aspect to funding and administration, there are few requirements from the state governments for German HEIs to engage with the regions. In sum, although HEIs are funded and administered at the level of the *Länder*, the Humboldtian tradition of German universities affords them a significant amount of autonomy.

At the regional level, there need to be incentives and funding programmes which encourage activity within HEIs which have an explicit regional dimension and aim to strengthening co-operative activity within the region. This is particularly important considering that for many HEIs, activities which encourage regional engagement are funded outwith core HE budgets.

However, it is likely that there would be little support from individual HEIs to increase a nationally planned system of HE at the regional level. This stems, in part, from an acknowledgement that regional contexts vary significantly and that individual HEIs must develop strategies appropriate to their own context rather than centrally imposed mechanisms.

In the United Kingdom, funding councils have been established in each of its constituent parts – the Higher Education Funding Council for England (HEFCE), the Scottish Higher Education Funding Council (SHEFC), the Higher Education Funding Council for Wales (HEFCW), and the Department of Education Northern Ireland (DENI). These structures are part of a wider process of political and administrative devolution occurring in the regions of the United Kingdom. Many of these funding councils cover small coherent territories, for example HEFCW includes the 13 HEIs in Wales and DENI covers the two universities in Northern Ireland – Queens and Ulster.

In the case of HEFCE, Regional Officers have been established to provide strategic guidance to HEIs at a regional level and to collaborate over several regional based initiatives in England. Further, the Department for Education and Employment finances the HE Regional Development fund (HERD) which aims to increase the contribution of HEIs to regional competitiveness and to local or regional labour markets. The fund covers over 50 projects and fosters partnerships between HE, employers, Training and Enterprise Councils (TECs), regional government offices involved in raising regional skills.

4

Characteristics of the Region

How higher education institutions respond to regional needs, and indeed what are perceived as regional needs, will also be influenced by the characteristics of the region. HEIs therefore need to develop a collective understanding of the characteristics of their region, or regions, in order to identify particular opportunities for engagement. An analysis of the strengths and weaknesses of the regional context for HEIs is an important preliminary step to meaningful engagement and should include a number of aspects which are discussed below.

The nature of the region and the regional stakeholders

♦ What are the characteristics of the region in terms of its economic base, cultural activity, employment structure and levels of entrepreneurial activity and civic networks?
♦ What are the characteristics of the regional institutional networks and what "lead" or regulating agencies exist?
♦ What expectations do regional stakeholders voice to HEIs?

Understanding the characteristics of the region is of fundamental importance to active and meaningful university-regional engagement. A typology of regions can be constructed which groups together regions in terms of the types of problems they may face and the solutions they may seek. Davies (1997) identified four different regional types within which the higher education system can fulfil a different role:

• Low Income, Stagnant Region   • Low Income, Growth Region
• High Income, Stagnant Region   • High Income, Growth Region

Further, the Association of European Universities (CRE) created a three-region typology to identify different contexts for university-regional dialogues. These included regions of concentration (high levels of economic and educational development), regions of economic revival (re-emergence of previously strong regions after decades of relative decline) and peripheral regions (rural or marginal regions) (see Davies, 1998). Of particular interest are regions in transition such as those in the post-communist world which face a number of specific challenges such as on-going economic and political restructuring.

HEI policy makers and managers, then, need to be aware of the significant differences which exist between, and within, regions in terms of composition of industrial sectors, public and private employment structures, levels of entrepreneurial activity, SME growth, population density and growth, social service provision, educational provision, the nature of local co-operation and civic traditions, quality of life and cultural activity.

It is also vital to understand the character and number of stakeholders in the region. The term "stakeholder" refers to those organisations or individuals in the region who interact, or have the potential to interact, with the higher education sector. This "regional cluster" is comprised of several groups:

- The educational sector including schools, further education (FE) and higher education (HE).
- Business and industrial community and privately run research activity.
- Support organisations such as trade unions, regional development, inward investment and promotional organisations, chambers of commerce.
- Local and regional governments.
- Educational users embracing a range of learners from full-time students to those participating in continuing professional courses and non-accredited liberal adult education.

Establishing relationships between HEIs and regional stakeholders can be problematic for several reasons. Firstly, if greater collaboration between HEIs and other agencies is going to be achieved then mismatches in investment cycles and delivery times will have to be addressed. The first of these is the time scale on which HEIs on the one hand, and companies on the other, conduct their business. By and large HEIs are locked into annual cycles for their teaching and for their decision-making processes and the output of their graduates, whereas companies may need faster decisions and delivery.

Secondly, it is often difficult for the region's industry to represent a "sector of interests" to HEIs. This is enhanced in fragmented and peripheral economic regions characterised by contracting and declining local industry, externally-managed branch plants and difficult to reach SMEs which represent a diverse interest group. Communication between HEIs and regional stakeholders can be improved where there exists lead agencies for various sectors such as local economic development, employment, culture, health, etc.

Thirdly, it is crucial to appreciate that organisations involved in promoting regional economic development such as local and regional governments, regional promotional agencies and chambers of commerce, function within explicitly defined areas. In contrast, HEIs have always operated as mediating institutions between several different geographical scales which range from the local to the global. HEIs, then, face a number of "positioning" challenges in terms of balancing its territorial interest with those of its regional partners.

New forms of regional governance and policy

- ◆ What are the main drivers of regional policy and what regional policy mechanisms and funding opportunities exist which offer selective financial assistance and funds to promote economic development?
- ◆ To what extent is there a tradition of co-ordinated and coherent regional government?
- ◆ What formal and informal mechanisms exist in the region to promote regional co-operation and partnerships?

As noted earlier, regions are becoming increasingly important arenas for economic, social, cultural activity and new sets of administrative, organisational and institutional practices are being put in place to which HEIs have to respond. This "new regionalism" is being superimposed in states with long established differences in the degrees of political decentralisation which may or may not incorporate higher education.

Many countries, such as the United States, Australia and a number of continental European countries, have a strong tradition of decentralisation and civic responsibility whilst others, such as the United Kingdom and Scandinavian countries have a much stronger legacy of centralised control. Where regional mechanisms are, as yet, poorly developed, the regional agenda being pursued by many higher education institutions may be occurring in a national policy vacuum. In Europe this vacuum is being filled by the European Commission. The following section discusses developments in the European Union, to explore a context which is rapidly expanding an organisational capacity for regional governance and policy within which the regional management of HEIs can grow.

A Europe of the regions

A major driver to greater HEI-region engagement in most parts of Europe has been the existence of the European Union (EU) and its various policy mechanisms. While there are many national differences, in the status, funding and organisation, of the HE sector and a great diversity of individual HEIs, in terms of institutional history and culture, there are a number of common pressures which are creating a new framework for HEIs throughout the EU.

The Maastricht Treaty sets out a vision for Europe as a "Europe of the regions". Within this framework of Maastricht, political regions were enshrined in EU primary law and gain representation through the Committee of the Regions with regional actors institutionalised within its political-legal system. Regionalism is a unifying rather than fragmentary force within the overall framework of Europe and functions as a third tier of governance below the EU and the nation-state. The Assembly of European Regions was created in 1993 comprised of 237 regions to become the most important body representing regional interests in Europe. This framework of legally recognised regions has given rise to cross-border co-operation in "Euro-regions". There is also co-

33

operation between non-contiguous EU regions which express common strategic aims or similar socio-economic problems.

A process of economic regionalisation is occurring in conjunction with this political regionalisation of the EU, which, however, is less explicitly associated with defined political units. An elaborate regional economic policy framework has developed to support the ability of regions to adapt to structural economic change in the wake of the declining effectiveness of national and macro-economic regulation. This process of economic regionalisation is situated within the wider processes of political and economic deregulation and the declining regulatory capabilities of the nation-state as highlighted in Chapter 2. The growth of cross-border relations gives credence to new geographical patterns of economic activity which highlight the resurgence of the region and the decline of the nation-state. European Economic and Monetary Union (EMU) is a fundamental aspect of the economic regionalisation process within which countries must fulfil certain convergence criteria in order to participate in monetary union. These political and economic drivers towards regionalisation are strengthened by cultural impulses associated with the expression of strong regional identities and tensions between ethnic, language and cultural groups within certain EU nation-states.

European integration, then, opens up new possibilities for regional independence and new forms of responsibility at the regional level. However, the ability of various regions to respond to these economic and political transformations is highly variable and is influenced by existing infrastructures of collaboration and leadership mechanisms, the characteristics of the economic base and its physical and strategic location within the European and global economy. In this sense, despite regional policy measures, there still exists central regions in Europe which occupy a dominant position and inhibit the wholesale convergence of core and peripheral regions.

The regionalisation process varies by character and degree across the various member states of the EU. Many economically and politically weak regions suffer from a lack of regional co-operation, strong regional actors and regional self-determination, whilst other regions have a deeply embedded sense of regionalism. For example, Germany's system of *Länder* are the strongest sub-national units in the EU and have a state-like quality. Spain also has, within a spectrum of regional governments, a sub-group of strong autonomous regions based upon separatist claims by nationalist groups in areas such as Catalonia and the Basque Country. Moreover, the most autonomous communities in Spain have a significant amount of power and resemble the German *Länder*. Belgium exhibits tendencies towards confederation to accommodate the long standing conflict between the Flemish and Walloon regions. In France, regions only have limited power, especially in terms of finances. Less clear impulses to regionalism are seen in other EU states such as Denmark, Finland, Greece, Ireland, Luxembourg, the Netherlands, Portugal and Sweden where a recent referendum rejected the spread of regional autonomy from the Azores and Madeira to also apply on the mainland.

The United Kingdom represents an interesting case within the EU framework due to its continued ambivalence towards some aspects of the EU policy framework, especially monetary union, and its recent experimentation with devolution and regional mechanisms. Historically, the United Kingdom government has been largely inimical to the idea of regional government and has approached regional development through a patchwork of uncoordinated mechanisms. However, co-ordinated regionalism and devolution is gaining momentum in the United Kingdom, not least because of the establishment of parliaments for Scotland and Northern Ireland and a Welsh Assembly, but also because of the move towards regional bodies within the English regions and an elected mayor and assembly for London. Overall, these changes will have an important constitutional impact over the whole of the United Kingdom.

If one considers the constituent parts of the United Kingdom, it is evident that regionalism is unfolding in a slow, multi-stage process in England in contrast to more rapid progress in Scotland, Northern Ireland and Wales. The original vision of the new Labour government to promote elected regional assemblies in English regions which had sufficient public demand was seen as a way of compensating for the long-standing democratic deficit within England. This route has been moderated and the chosen option set out in the government White Paper *Building Partnerships for Prosperity: Sustainable Growth, Competitiveness and Employment in the English Regions* (DETR, 1997) involves the creation of indirectly elected regional chambers based on existing regional associations of local authorities and Regional Development Agencies (RDAs) in each English region to act as the executive arm of the chambers. It is the RDAs which now form the core of the government's approach to regionalism in England. They have a clear role in providing a strategic framework for the actions of the numerous stakeholders, including higher education, in economic, social and political development process at a regional scale.

The White Paper which sets out a vision for the RDAs recognises that HE plays a key economic role at the regional level, both in terms of direct employment and spending and indirect impacts through knowledge and skills generation. Moreover, in relation to enhancing skills, the role of the RDAs is to ensure that educational programmes in the region are fully integrated with the needs of the region. Regional stakeholders in England, then, such as local government, Training and Enterprise Councils (TECs), government offices for the regions, chambers of commerce, FE and HE sector, inward investment and Regional Development Agencies are all increasingly focusing their efforts explicitly on local and regional economic development. The challenge is the extent to which the new tier of the RDAs can co-ordinate policy at a regional level to enhance regional convergence within England.

A key player in many of the emerging developments around the changing role of regions within Europe, and the need for new structures to effect economic development strategies has been the European Union through its concern for economic and social cohesion. A wide variety of EU policy mechanisms exist to promote economic development, educational provision and skills training at the regional level which promote the mobilisation of regional actors. The EU seeks to reduce regional disparities across member states through the European Structural Funds, notably the European Regional Development Fund (ERDF) established in

1975 to reduce the differences in development between the various regions within the EU, especially the southern Mediterranean countries which contained severely lagging regions, and the European Social Fund (ESF) which exists to improve employment prospects in the EU.

Many HEIs participate in both ERDF and ESF projects aimed at enhancing local skills or assisting local SMEs to develop in capability or technological sophistication. Since the 1980s, there has been an increased orientation of ERDF support towards the encouragement of innovation in SMEs and underpinning R-D capability from regional HEIs. However, more importantly with regard to the emerging regional governance of the Structural Funds, a number of schemes funded under Article 10 of the ERDF regulation have been launched, with the purpose of developing regional level strategies in fields such as innovation and information society. HEIs have been major players in these strategic reviews, often providing research inputs as well as having involvement in steering committees and expert panels.

The accumulation of expertise in such localised interactions is leading to the emergence of European-wide consortia of HEIs in order to exploit possibilities opened up by the EU to contribute to regional economic growth. For example, the European Consortium of Innovative Universities (ECIU) has been established with 10 partner institutions. ECIU partners, many of which are discussed below, are particularly interested in stimulating regional development by encouraging technology transfer and greater co-operation between universities and SMEs. ECIU is currently collaborating with the European Commission's Innovation Programme to study further issues of technology transfer.

An important context for this regional level activity however is the globalisation and networking of European education, partly through the impact of the information society on HEIs and research. New divisions of academic labour may be developing, with important implications for the roles played by HEIs in regional development. In particular, the emergence of "academic Euro-regions" which span national boundaries, introduces interesting territorial questions for the governance of HEIs in Europe. Moreover, the long-term effects of the move towards a future European (virtual?) university and the provision of education by global actors outwith the EU also need to be examined.

5

Institutional Management
for Regional Engagement

The implications of the dynamics between globalisation, regionalisation and localisation that have been outlined have yet to be addressed by most HEIs. Responding to this changing external environment requires the establishment of management interfaces to steer HEIs in new ways.

This chapter highlights a number of management strategies which are being employed by HEIs to engage with the region. These include evaluating and mapping the regional impacts of HEIs; assessing their institutional capacity to engage with the region; creating a new organisational culture and mechanisms to facilitate communication on regional issues within HEIs and between HEIs and other regional stakeholders; and, finally, new forms of financial management. These new forms of management span the three core functions of HEIs – teaching, research, and community service.

Evaluating and mapping the impact of the regional HE system

- ♦ Has the HEI undertaken an audit of its impacts and links with the region?
- ♦ How are such impact statements used and distributed to the region and further afield to promote the HEI and the region?
- ♦ Do mechanisms exist to raise awareness of the role of the HEI in the region?

At a regional level, there is a deficit of systematically collected information concerning the role of HEIs in regional development. In the light of this, HEIs, in partnership with other regional stakeholders, need to embark upon an evaluation and mapping process to assess the broad range of impacts and roles which they have in the region. The most useful format for such an evaluation process involves collaboration between all the HEIs in a region and other regional stakeholders to establish a steering group which can formulate guidelines and monitor regional engagement. Moreover, a lead agency is required to act as an advisory body to facilitate this process. Such a reflective and mutual evaluation process will be new to most regions and can be used as a frame of reference for future evaluations.

The aim of such an evaluation process is to bring together HEIs and other regional partners, through workshops and seminars, to identify areas of interaction and non-interaction. In general, this process is an exercise to increase mutual understanding concerning those involved in the regional development process and to raise awareness of the activities of HEIs in the region. It is also important for HEIs to increase institutional self-awareness in terms of disseminating knowledge concerning how the institution works and the extent of its links in the region.

Underpinning such an evaluation is the issue of why the institution is embarking upon increased regional engagement. HEIs must ensure that increased regional engagement adds to, rather than detracts from, its reputation in teaching and research. In this way, regional engagement should be selective and focused and should be a response to genuine needs identified in the region.

A recent useful example of the process of self-evaluating of the regional role of universities came from the Finnish Higher Education Evaluation Council which guided a self-assessment exercise concerning the three universities in Eastern Finland. These self-evaluation reports were reflective and critical and were very profitable exercises for the universities involved. They are a useful complement to the more functional rank-based evaluation of government teaching and research assessments.

Underpinning the evaluation process is the need to identify and map the various impacts which HEIs have in the region. A number of techniques can be used to highlight these impacts. It is essential to establish the "counter-factual"; in other words, what would the region be like if the HEIs did not exist. It is clear that most municipalities regard HEIs as an overall positive influence. There may be a stronger tradition of HEIs in peripheral or declining areas disseminating information on their regional impacts in order to boost or transform the image of the region and to induce migration and stem out-migration. However, it is important that HEIs and other regional stakeholders do not regard the institutions as a panacea to all manner of problems faced by the region.

Impacts which HEIs have in the region range from "passive" such as income and employment generation and contributions to the physical environment to "dynamic" such as network building, skills development and raising educational aspirations and creativity. The nature of impacts will be determined, in part, by factors such as discipline mix, size of institution and territorial focus. HEIs and regional partners undertaking an evaluation of the regional HE system need to explore the following areas.

Institutional evolution

What are the historic links between the HEI and the region and how have these developed? How has the institution evolved in terms of:
- Staff and student numbers.
- Faculty mix.
- Place of the institution in the regional and national higher education systems.

- Balance between teaching and research functions.
- Territorial focus?

HEIs of different levels of maturity display different priorities and different levels of regional engagement. For example, many smaller, specialist, predominantly teaching and regionally based institutions often develop more national and research functions as they mature.

Direct economic impact of institution

HEIs can claim a significant direct economic impact in the region through direct and indirect employment generation, staff and student spending and central purchasing. Students and staff recruited from outside the region are a net addition to the regional economy. Further, in relation to employment change in the region, HE employment may be growing whilst other sectors such as manufacturing and agriculture are declining. Such growth rates within the HE sector can be particularly important for countries experiencing economic restructuring to offset large scale employment loss in manufacturing industries. For example, in Australia, the HE system is the largest national export industry, exceeding traditionally strong sectors such as agriculture.

Table 1. **Multiplier values and employment impact derived from HEI impact studies in the United Kingdom**

University (date of study)	Multiplier value	Employment impact (direct and indirect)
Stirling University (1974)	1.24-1.54	1 600-3 100
Yorkshire and Humberside HEIs (1981)	1.3	55 600
University of East Anglia (1982)	1.2	2 857-3 057
Bristol Polytechnic (1982)	1.15	3 128
Coventry Polytechnic (1988)	1.5	2 400
Southampton University (1991)	1.197	4 913
Liverpool John Moores University (1993)	1.45	6 285

Source: Goddard *et al.* (1994).

It was calculated that in 1995/96, higher education in the United Kingdom generated employment for over 3% of the total United Kingdom workforce and the gross output generated by it was over £43 billion (McNicoll *et al.*, 1997).

Direct economic impacts have been measured by numerous HEIs using Keynesian multiplier analysis. Such analysis is based upon the assumption that initial injections of expenditure into HEIs lead to expenditure in the region by that institution which leads to subsequent rounds of expenditure by those benefiting from this expenditure and so on. Multipliers are calculated from these rounds of expenditure and vary according to the size of the region, leakages, level of taxation and so on. The size of multipliers varies, but most HEI impact studies have assumed them to be around 1.5.

Economic impact studies are a useful starting point to establish the impact of HEIs in the region. They have been used to highlight the scale of income and employment generation in a defined area as a result of the presence of HEIs. Numerous existing studies exist which can be used as a framework for such analysis. Studies from several British universities have revealed significant local income and employment effects from the presence of HEIs (Table 1).

Contributions to local economic development

The impact of HEIs in regional development also goes beyond these economic impacts and embraces more dynamic effects associated with enhancing the stock of skills and knowledge within a region. Examples include technology transfer to industry; recruiting students from outwith the region and placing them with local companies; the flow of staff and students into the regional labour market; programmes of continuing and professional development to enhance the skills of local managers; raising skills and educational levels in the region; locally embedding global businesses by targeted training programmes and research links; and providing a gateway to the global knowledge base for SMEs.

Social and cultural impact

HEIs fulfil wider social and cultural roles in the region by providing media expertise and commentary, access to public lectures and facilities, providing key leaders for local civil society, offering impartial knowledge to regional organisations and promoting the region and contributing to inward investment.

There is an important impact from HEIs, their staff and students, in terms of promoting regional cultural vitality and innovation. HEIs provide significant local audiences for regional arts and culture activities and their presence contributes to a virtuous cycle of growth between cultural consumption and production for example, by sustaining audience levels at certain venues which may in turn offer HEIs resources for teaching and research. Art and cultural activities which are sustained by the presence of HEIs contribute to the broadening of perspectives within the region. HEIs, then, are a gateway to the wider economic, social and cultural world, which can be of vital importance in the development of peripheral and marginal regions.

Capacity building for regional co-operation

♦ Does the HEI recognise that by its very nature the territorial development process is broadly based, embracing economic, technology, environmental, social, cultural and political agendas?
♦ Does the HEI have adequate mechanisms in place to engage successfully with the region?
♦ Has the catalyst for regional engagement been internal or external to the HEI?

An important element of the self-evaluation process is to assess the institution's current and potential "capacity" for engaging with regional stakeholders and the regional development process. It is often observed that the traditional values and collegial governance models of HEIs are not effective mechanisms for increasing regional engagement. The institutional characteristics of academic organisations are, in general, different to other institutions, especially in terms of their ability to adapt to a changing environment. In particular, a prerequisite for effective interaction between HEIs and regional stakeholders is that the institutional culture of HEIs bear some similarity to that of its partners. However, HEIs are complex, and often locally disembedded, organisations and as a result have to develop additional, externally-focused, organisational units in order to interact with regional stakeholders.

There are many impediments, then, to fostering greater regional engagement amongst HEIs, especially with regard to older and more well established universities. The ability, and desire, to encourage regional engagement is influenced by a whole host of factors such as the subject mix, the curriculum, the traditions of HEI-regional relationships and the history of co-operation within the region. However, in a recent series of case studies of the characteristics of the "entrepreneurial" university a number of themes have been identified which point to ways in which certain HEIs have been able to transform themselves. These include (Clark, 1998):

• A strengthened steering core.
• An expanded development periphery (research centres, science parks, etc.).
• A diversified funding base.
• A stimulated academic heartland.
• A new institutional idea.

Interestingly, this list does not include "regional engagement" as one of the characteristics of a transformed HEI; however, careful reading of the case studies does indeed suggest that greater interaction with the surrounding environment has been a significant way through which HEIs have transformed themselves into entrepreneurial and responsive institutions.

OECD 1999

The transformation process within HEIs, especially the older universities, is *interactive* and *incremental* in nature (Clark, 1998) and so developing capacities for regional responsiveness requires a long-term and multi-faceted approach. The infrastructure of a regionally responsive HEI, then, has a number of basic characteristics such as financial and management deregulation and decentralisation backed by a strengthened, flexible and streamlined management core; the establishment of horizontal support units; and "short-lines" of communication between individual units and university managers. Efficient and effective management processes are a necessary precondition for successful regional engagement. Moreover, explicit incentives and mechanisms are needed to mainstream regional considerations within the institution such as the representation of external bodies in internal decision making in order that regional priorities can be channelled to the right places.

But the obstacles to change should not be underestimated. Many larger and older HEIs suffer from institutional sluggishness, lack the ability to experiment and demonstrate a slower capacity to respond to regional needs. Further, whilst the majority of activities within HEIs are disciplinary-based, many regional opportunities require interdisciplinary teaching and research. Departmental regroupings and new interdisciplinary units may therefore be necessary. Over and beyond such mechanisms for greater regional engagement, capacity building also requires changing the less tangible elements of the institution such as its values and social structure.

In short, improved integration of HEIs with regional development will not be readily achieved by top down planning mechanisms at either the institutional or regional level but by ensuring that the various stakeholders in the regional development process – education and training providers, employers and employers organisations, trade unions, economic development and labour market agencies and individual teachers and learners – have an understanding of each others roles and the factors encouraging or inhibiting greater regional engagement.

Creating a new organisational culture

The capacity of an HEI to meet regional needs may rest on its ability to adopt and embed new working practices. There are significant cultural obstacles to adopting greater regional engagement within HEIs partly because of the connotations which regionalism has with parochialism, newness and unsophistication. Whilst many senior managers may be willing to promote greater co-operation in research and teaching with local industry and local government, this opinion is not always transferred to academics at the department level.

A number of HEIs have literally created a new institutional idea to overcome embedded institutional practices which have blocked greater regional engagement and through this have built up a capacity to encourage greater institutional-wide regional engagement.

The University of Twente in the Netherlands took the strategic step in the 1980s to position itself as the "entrepreneurial university". This idea was enshrined through the establishment of the University of Twente Entrepreneurship Centre (UTEC) which brings together activities in the field of entrepreneurship from across the university. UTEC includes a Research Centre, Training Centre, Teaching Centre and Technology Transfer Centre. This new entrepreneurial idea for the university has created a new organisational culture, defined by an attitude for taking risks.

The University of Strathclyde in Scotland has adopted the phrase "a place of useful learning." This idea for the institution draws upon its historical strength as a practical and locally relevant institution but also gives the university a new cohesive identity. Strathclyde uses this idea to project a university-wide image that it is always ready to increase links with local industry.

Warwick University in the West Midlands in the United Kingdom was established in 1965 as part of new breed of universities in Britain which were, to a certain extent, allowed to create their own image. It was unique in that from its inception it did not have a plan and academics had a large degree of autonomy to decide upon the nature of the institution. At Warwick, teaching and learning were research-led from the start, which attracted academics who had frequently been stifled by institutional practices at older universities. Close links with industry, including local industry became a central theme in its emerging vision.

Mechanisms to promote university-regional involvement

- ♦ To what extent has academic leadership and central management been altered to engage with regional needs?
- ♦ What are the main channels of communication between regional stakeholders and HEIs (senior managers, committees, etc.) and who is responsible for regional decisions in the institution?
- ♦ What internal mechanisms exist for co-ordinating regional activities within HEIs especially in relation to funding issues and what new posts/offices have been created with an explicitly regional local remit?
- ♦ In what ways are HEIs responding to regional ICT infrastructures and are they adopting new technologies to restructure their own management structures?
- ♦ How can the regional dimension be incorporated into the staff development policy of HEIs?
- ♦ What training should staff with regional responsibilities be given? How can staff be rewarded for regional engagement?

There is little doubt that relations with the region are regarded with some importance by many HEIs. However, the priority attached to this element in institutional plans varies significantly. Various internal mechanisms to co-ordinate regional activities such as policy and resources committees, heads of department forums, electronic discussion lists, special committees and senior management team meetings have been established. However, in many cases, responsibility for regional engagement rests with a small number of senior managers (vice-chancellors, rectors, presidents) and is not embedded into mainstream academic life, especially at the department level. The challenge faced by most HEIs is to create mechanisms which allow information about regional engagement to flow up and down the institutional hierarchy. Further, channels of communication, which involve the local media, need to be established which regularly report on HEI-regional engagement. Examples of good practice also need to be disseminated throughout the institution. The following section discusses various mechanisms which have emerged at various HEIs.

The role of central management

A problem which many HEIs face is a low ability to provide strong steering due to their dispersed and open institutional form. Problems of inefficient university management, arising especially from multiple committee structures, are evident in HEIs across many national contexts and were highlighted in Britain by the Jarrett Report (1985). Creating a strengthened, and smaller, central administration is a vital element in guiding regional involvement. However, such changes involve conflict between new managerial/entrepreneurial values and traditional academic values. Any attempts to alter management practices within HEIs have to compete with challenges from more collegiate and autonomous forms of academic leadership.

Some of the emerging models of HEI management can be encapsulated in the phrase "centralised decentralisation" (Clark, 1998) which represent a strong centre with short lines of communication to departmental units. Many HEIs are involved in transforming their central administration to respond to the changing external environment and regional needs.

The University of Strathclyde in Scotland was characterised by the absence of a central administrative core and was steered by over 50 central committees with most power resting with the Academic Planning Committee of 20 members. Steps were taken to overcome this inefficiency by radically reducing the number of university committees. The university established the University Management Group (UMG) comprised of about 10 members (5 deans, 5 senior managers) and which was independent from both Senate and Court. UMG provides a forum where managerial and academic values are used to steer the university. This structure was strengthened by a unified position of university Secretary which eliminated the posts of registrar and bursar.

Warwick University in Britain strengthened and centralised its administrative core and created a more direct relationship with department level units. A number of central steering committees bring together individual academics and senior officers without an intermediating faculty tier. Faculty and dean level tiers are absent and a flat management structure exists between departments and the administrative core. However, this centralised management structure is now coming under pressure as the university grows larger and more complex.

Internal mechanisms for regional engagement

Establishing a number of internal mechanisms which mediate between HEIs and the external environment is a key element of the regionally responsive HEI. Such mechanisms represent horizontal mechanisms which span the traditional vertical hierarchy of HEI structures. Such interfaces help to overcome one of the most significant problems facing HEIs in a regional context – their perception as a closed door or black box.

This perceptual problem can be overcome by establishing single entry-points or front-door mechanisms. These have taken various forms such as Regional Offices, City Offices, Research and Development Offices, International Offices, and External Liaison Offices, all of which are a growing element and can make a contribution towards meeting regional needs and creating an institutional capacity to respond. The remit of these new roles and offices has often been concerned with new funding opportunities, at the regional, national and supra-national level. Increasingly, there are examples of entry-point mechanisms which provide comprehensive access and information to the three roles of HEIs – teaching, research and service – embracing activities such as R-D, business services, student volunteering, learning opportunities, and academic, social and cultural events. There is an added-value to having single entry-points to HEIs in that there is the possibility that enquirers may find out about associated activities within the institution.

The University of Sheffield in Northern England has established a Regional Office to act as a one-stop-shop for all those wishing to access the university. The Regional Office co-ordinates student project work in the community, tackles access to higher education, and runs several business sector networks in the areas of material science, medicine and the environment. Further, the university helped to establish the City Liaison Group which developed economic and social regeneration plans for the city. The Regional Office is an unequivocal statement that the university is committed to the region. It is also an attempt to build a stronger relationship with the regional community, especially in the light of the severe levels of economic restructuring which the South Yorkshire region faces.

In Eastern Finland, Centres for continuing education within each university are responsible for co-ordinating education and business education and services to the regional population and act as catalysts for regional development projects. The centres offer a number of services which include continuing and adult education and open university studies especially to rural communities; labour market training through tailored professional education and management courses such as leadership training programmes and MBAs; and the co-ordination of development services and projects for the region. The centres liaise with numerous regional bodies such as the AMK institutions or "polytechnics", local industry and local government. One important aspect of work at the centres is developing East-West relations and collaborative projects with Russia.

The University of Leeds in Northern England has established the City and Regional Office which acts as a central mechanism to ensure that the university makes a full contribution to the city and region. It brings together several areas of interface which include links with local schools and colleges to widen access to the university and utilises existing students as mentors; community links which engage non-traditional students and inner-city communities in the work of the university; a range of facilities and services to support local business; and the City and Regional Initiative on Student Projects (CRISP) in which students carry out regionally-based project work.

The Liaison Group (LG) was established at the University of Twente in the Netherlands in 1996 as the central co-ordinating office for technology transfer. LG exists to build an effective bridge between the needs of industry and the university's research effort, and to act as the university "gateway" to education and training for the business community and the public sector. LG is supported by an advisory group comprised of regional members. LG co-ordinates entrepreneurial activity at the university which includes contract research, continuing professional development (CPD), business development, new innovative entrepreneurship and other projects linked to regional development. However, because of the success of these various initiatives, the sphere of LG is national rather than simply regional. The university also established UT-Extra which operates as a private foundation to encourage entrepreneurial activity throughout the university. This foundation was established as Dutch law inhibits universities from being involved in excessive forms of entrepreneurial activity.

Various mediums have been employed to communicate the regional role of HEIs to the community. These include new technologies such as e-mail and Internet resources and more traditional communication channels such as the print and visual media and radio. Radio stations have been used for many years as an interface between HEIs and the local community. Although such enterprises are often initially small in scale, many have grown and have been established on a commercial basis operating within a wider area. Student radio also acts as a vehicle for training in broadcast media and as an intermediate step into careers in the cultural industries.

The three regional universities and other educational institutions in Eastern Finland operate Radio Kantti, which is housed at the University of Kuopio and licensed by the Finnish Broadcasting Corporation. Radio Kantti plays a role in encouraging communication between and within institutions and offering training in broadcasting activities. The radio station is also utilised in supporting employment, job placements and a way to internationalisation.

At the University of Newcastle in Northern England, a campus based radio station, Ice FM, was established in 1994. Subsequently, the radio station has expanded out of the university and has begun to operate regionally. Ice FM has been one of the central components in promoting cultural activities, especially those relating to dance and music cultures, in the region and stages various musical events in the city which are attended by students and non-students alike.

The regional information and communication technology infrastructure

It is vital to consider the implication of information and communication technologies (ICTs) in the evolving debate concerning the transformation of HEIs. ICTs are being shaped within HEIs, and, in turn, are contributing to the re-shaping of higher education. In particular, new technological initiatives are changing HEIs as social institutions and they are reworking the very way in which they operate. HEIs are often at the leading edge of technological developments, and can provide important insights into the development of the virtual society, especially at a regional level.

ICTs are being utilised to enhance regional networks, which have the potential to enhance the regional development process. HEIs can play a central role within the development of these regional ICT networks in several ways. Firstly, they can become involved in establishing and developing advanced technical infrastructures which connects the regional academic community. Secondly, they can provide skilled staff who are involved in the implementation of ICT strategies. Thirdly, they can act as partners within the development of regional information systems and offer services such as video conferencing, computer archiving and databanks and multi-media courses based around the virtual campus. Finally, HEIs can act as neutral brokers to promote debate concerning the implications of the introduction of new technologies. In sum, by their very nature, HEIs can play a central role in shaping the evolution of information society at a regional level.

More specifically, some HEIs have become heavily involved in the establishment of Metropolitan Area Networks (MANS) which link together educational institutions and other stakeholders within a particular region. The MANs being established in the HEI sector are able to deliver a broadband capacity

(34Mbps and increasingly 155Mbps) infrastructure which can provide innovative applications such as distance learning, high quality image transfers, access to remote facilities and video. They also give credence to concepts such as the "virtual university", especially in terms of promoting study in geographically remote areas and the delivery of flexible lifelong learning.

MANs mainly exist to encourage collaborative local and regional partnerships between HEIs. However, they also have the potential to facilitate partnerships with the local and regional community as access is expanded to further education institutions, schools, industry and domestic users. It is important that regional ICT infrastructures are developed collaboratively between several regional stakeholders to avoid duplication of effort. The potential contribution of technical infrastructures such as MANs to regional development is determined by the ability to extend access to them, and in particular, to the teaching and research facilities of the regional HEIs connected to such networks. Although many of the technical developments within MANs are impressive, there are dangers that the benefits largely accrue to the academic and research communities.

In the North West England, G-MING exists to create a high performance multi-service telecommunication infrastructure for the Greater Manchester higher educational community and to explore the possibilities of collaboration with other organisations (research units, FE colleges, libraries, hospitals, schools, high-tech businesses) in the region. Partly funded by the European Regional Development Fund (ERDF), the G-MING project covers 32 sites including the 5 major HEIs in the city, 4 teaching medical institutes, several halls of residence and city council sites.

One of the aims of G-MING is to enable resources and network connections (*e.g.* SuperJANET) to be shared between organisations in a more cost-effective manner and to extend the facilities out to remote sites (such as halls of residence) in order to promote changes in social and organisational practice (*e.g.* teleworking, distance learning). It is also hoped that service provision can be extended to other non academic organisations and thereby take on a wider role in support of the economic regeneration of the Greater Manchester area.

HEIs, then, because of their expertise in the installation and development of technical infrastructures, often act as co-ordinators and facilitators in regional information networks which draw together various stakeholders to improve the exchange of information and knowledge throughout the region. The aim and effectiveness of such networks to the regional development process is a reflection of the technical competence of those involved, the priorities of those partners engaged in such networks, and the dedication amongst the partners to increasing network access.

The Polytechnic University of Catalonia (UPC) in Spain is leading a project which aims to create a powerful telematic service network capable of increasing enterprise creation opportunities through a virtual business incubator. It is hoped that the project will allow regional actors to accumulate know-how through networked service provision and technology transfer and attract to the region actors involved in powerful telematic service networks. As a result of these growing telematic networks, the school of multimedia was established at the Terrassa campus of UPC with the direct support of a multinational company.

A major region-wide strategy for the development of the information society is being developed in the North-East region of England. This is being undertaken within the framework of the Regional Information Society Initiative (RISI) which is funded partly by the EU and regional partners and involves the universities, local authorities and Training and Enterprise Councils. The project is being managed by the Northern Informatics Application Agency (NiAA), a non-profit making company run by the private and public sectors; a number of the regional universities played a leading role in its establishment. The aim of NiAA is to raise awareness, understanding and skills in the area of telematics and to work with telecommunication network suppliers to upgrade the communications infrastructure of the region.

ICT networks of this nature are part of the research landscape across the world and there are moves to connect separate national networks together to create a "network of networks" throughout large parts of the world. In Europe, for example, several initiatives exist to promote a pan-European ICT network for European researchers by connecting national research networks.

Clearly, the implications of the introduction of new technological infrastructures throw up a number of challenges and potentials which are only beginning to be contemplated by HEIs and other regional partners. In particular, there are important issues concerning major shifts in working practices, the erosion of institutional sovereignty and ensuring equitable access to technological networks. Further, while participation in ICT networks and information society projects is a necessary condition for the creation of a learning region, there is always the danger that the powerful forces of globalisation that are unleashed will undermine fledgling intra-regional processes of collaboration.

HEIs and management information systems

In addition to the changes occurring in the region's technological infrastructure, HEIs are also introducing new internal technical infrastructures and software applications. These new management information systems (MIS) are contributing to widespread institutional change in relation to administration, teaching, research and marketing. Such systems are an essential component of the regionally responsive and entrepreneurial HEI. The introduction of new internal MIS, can therefore support new forms of management and communication within HEIs and thereby have the potential to reconfigure its relationship with regional stakeholders. More specifically, data capture is an enterprise-wide component of MIS and concerns patterns of regional engagement (student origins, work placements, graduate destinations, industrial contracts) which can be used in self-evaluation and performance monitoring and to assist with identifying potential collaborators both within the HEI and from outside. In short, the MIS, notwithstanding the cultural shifts involved in its introduction, are a necessary tool to support effective regional engagement.

Incentives and reward structures for regional engagement

It is widely recognised that the loyalty of many academics is to their discipline rather than their institution. Moreover, the current system of peer review through, for example, scholarly and nationally/internationally focused publications, can discourage active regional engagement amongst staff. To overcome the barriers requires active staff development programmes which promote knowledge of the region and skills for working with external partners. Appraisal processes and senior management development programmes are useful tools to monitor, reward and promote regional activities. However, most HEIs devote limited resources to staff development and if they are to respond to new regionally based agendas they will need to enhance the skills and competencies of their staff at all levels and reward them accordingly.

At the Royal Melbourne Institute of Technology in Australia, all faculties are required to establish strategic activities and targets for community service. Further, staff promotion includes criteria involving community leadership and an annual award is granted for quality management of a community service project.

The University of Joensuu in Finland adopted a pilot scheme known as "flexible work loads". The idea of the system was that within a nationally set workload requirement of a certain amount of hours per year, staff could negotiate with their department the allocation of time between the four major tasks of education, research, public services and other responsibilities. This counteracts the tight government controls set on Finnish universities by the government and gives departments more freedom.

One of the main mechanisms to enable HEIs to meet regional needs are dedicated individuals with regional remits. Such people can be considered "animateurs" – individuals or groups of people who are pursuing new, often regionally focused, institutional ideas and working practices for the institution. Such individuals or groups are vital in several respects; they translate and embed new ideas into HEIs and they act as intermediaries who "lower the threshold" (Hölttä and Pulliainen, 1996) between practices in HEIs and in the world of business. Responding to regional needs is not just about developing communication channels but developing people whose role is to facilitate the communication process.

Promoting regional dialogue

♦ What mechanisms exist to promote communication and dialogue between HEIs and regional stakeholders?

♦ How can the regional interests of various sectors of interest such as HE, industry, the private, public and voluntary sectors be represented?

♦ What is the extent and nature of HEI staff representation on public/private bodies in the region?

♦ What are the reasons for such representation and what is their role?

♦ Is such representation monitored?

♦ What role do external bodies play in decision making within HEIs?

Communicating regional interests

Dialogue between HEIs and regional stakeholders depends upon adequate communication practices and networks. In many cases of HEI-regional relationships, there is often no clear set of assumptions from HEIs in terms of what the region needs apart from notions such as the region's companies would benefit from various forms of technological transfer and skills provision. Similarly, there are often no clear assumptions from regional bodies concerning the role of HEIs in the region except that HEIs are repositories of knowledge and expertise which should be conferred on the region wherever possible.

Relationships between HEIs and regions can be characterised by mutual confusion and often disinterestedness. Many HEIs, especially those which rely less upon local and regional funding sources, regard themselves as autonomous institutions with little regional accountability. Moreover, in cases where closer collaboration is sought, it is often difficult to identify a clear set of needs from the region, especially in a context which involves multiple partners and a range of activities.

Representation of regional interests to HEIs often operates on a scatter-gun basis and at an individual rather than strategic and institution level. In many cases, it is senior managers who are the main channel of communication. It is unclear how dialogue at lower levels is communicated upwards and downwards within HEIs. One important mechanism to increase the level of communication between HEIs and regional stakeholders is to enhance a "marketing culture" throughout the whole institution.

A recent survey of the United Kingdom universities found that there are significant differences between universities in the distribution of responsibility for the management of relationships with local and regional partners. It is clear that promoting regional activities remain principally a senior management task, guided by a special committee or the general university policy and resources committee. While there may be engagement at the level of the individual academic and/or department, there is limited evidence of a vertical linkage through the institution. The structures adopted by old universities might be regarded as supporting a tactical engagement with the local community while those adopted by new universities reflect a more strategic approach with more focused responsibility.

Many HEIs, in partnership with other regional stakeholders, are becoming more active in establishing regional fora to promote dialogue and co-operative activity.

In the North East of England, the University of Newcastle, along with the University of Northumbria at Newcastle, and two of the regional Training and Enterprise Councils (TECs) form the "Strategy for Co-Operation Management Group". This is becoming an effective springboard for collaboration in the region, and the group along with the North-East Chamber of Commerce are frequently key partners in funding proposals to regional and central government offices.

The city of Terrassa in Catalonia is home to the School and College of Industrial Engineering of the Polytechnic University of Catalonia (UPC) and a number of other university institutions. The Terrassa Strategic Plan (PECT) has been established by the city council which sets forth a collective strategy for the future of the city, part of which is to bring together these HEIs to promote a unified university campus in Terrassa. This campus will establish it as Catalonia's second university city after Barcelona and will create a two-way relationship between the city, the university and industry. Through PECT, the Terrassa University Forum was established to facilitate communication between the university institutions and local authorities and promote the city as a university town. A major urban development is proposed to create a urban university campus for UPC in Terrassa. In sum, PECT regards the growth of the university sector as one of the city's defining factors for the future.

There are also examples of HEIs establishing mechanisms for communication which reflect the inter-regional and inter-national nature of governance and territorial focus of stakeholders.

The French Ministry of Education and Research helped to establish a number of European Academic Networks which have created a partnership between HEIs, industry and political bodies in the French regions. One such European Academic Network, the *Pôle Universitaire Européen Lille Nord-Pas de Calais* brings together seven universities, two research institutes, local governments and chambers of commerce. The main aim of the network is to pursue international relations and communicate the role of the region to the outside world. Moreover, this network is at the forefront of developing a larger academic Euro-region which includes HEIs not only in the Nord-Pas de Calais region, but also in South-East England, and the Walloon, Brussels and Flanders regions of Belgium.

Monitoring HEI-regional representation

Greater HEI-regional interaction can be fostered by appointing regional representatives to the administrative bodies of HEIs. The charters of many HEIs, especially older universities, require formal (ex officio) representation of outside bodies such as local authorities, churches and trade unions. However, many newer and less tradition-bound HEIs prefer individual representation on their governing structures. In a recent survey of Nordic universities, it was found that this form of "social interaction" had a clear positive impact on the development of universities. It was also found that such social interaction with outside bodies allows universities to compete more favourably with other regional institutions.

> The University of Joensuu in Eastern Finland attempted to improve its responsiveness to regional needs by incorporating four external members onto Senate: two local mayors, the Director of the Association of regional municipalities and the managing director of the region's largest industrial firm. However, these members only have power to speak rather than full decision making powers. External representation is also found on the boards of the Karalian Research Institute, the Mekrijarvi Research Station and the continuing education centre at the university.

> Southern Cross University in Australia was required by legislature to have particular regard to the needs of the North coast region of the New South Wales region. Moreover, it is formally required to include "persons associated with the North coast region of the State" on its governing council and to enter into arrangements with other regional education providers.

At the same time, the staff of HEIs are also likely to be represented on regional bodies. This representation in the community exists in a variety of forms ranging from individual, ad-hoc and unmonitored personal engagement from university staff to regulated and official mechanisms. Many older universities have statutory appointment responsibilities in the region such as governorship of schools. Further, the growth of quangos (quasi autonomous, non-governmental organisations) has increased the number of positions to which senior HEI staff can be appointed.

It is difficult to gauge the extent to which HEIs permeate the region through such representation, but mechanisms need to be established to monitor the extent of external membership on local and regional organisations such as professional and learned bodies, health authorities, law and order organisations, trade unions, school governing boards, cultural venues, churches, local government committees, development agencies and chambers of commerce.

Financial management

- ♦ How should regional and national funding streams be managed? What are the possibilities of financial decentralisation within the institution?
- ♦ How can HEIs embed new devolved financial responsibilities into academic life?
- ♦ How can new resources for regional engagement and activity be generated?
- ♦ Who pays for the regional role of HEIs?
- ♦ What new regional funding streams are emerging which HEIs can tap into?
- ♦ What mechanisms are being established to tap into these sources?

Diversifying and devolving HEI funding

There is a noticeable trend within most higher education systems towards government financial support representing a declining proportion of total HEI funds. Many of the oldest universities in the world developed outside of state control and were established from finances derived from ecclesiastical patronage and local industrial benefactors. Over the course of this century, the state has adopted the role of paymaster and administrator of HE. However, in the last few decades several national governments have reduced their financial support for higher education which has forced HEIs to seek alternative funding sources.

This shift away from central government financial support highlights the extent to which the financial viability of HEIs is becoming dependent upon entrepreneurial activity to capture external funding including local and regional sources. A threefold typology of funding sources can be created to understand this shift.

Stream 1: Mainline state allocation

The first funding stream relates to government money allocated to HEIs based upon student numbers, space needs, etc. There are differences between national systems in terms of the ways in which government funds are allocated. In some countries funds are allocated on the basis of inputs (*i.e.* number of students enrolled) whilst in others, funds are distributed according to outputs (*i.e.* number of successful degrees). However, as a general rule HEIs are not funded on the basis of delivery of graduates into employment. Most national funding streams therefore do not incorporate any regional criteria and, as a result, do not promote or enhance the engagement of HEIs with their region. However, some governments, such as the autonomous regional governments in Spain are adopting contracting arrangements where specific deliverables relating to economic and social objectives are spelt out.

In Britain, central government funds are allocated by the Higher Education Funding Council for England (HEFCE) (or the Scottish Higher Education Funding Council in Scotland). HEFCE allocates funds to each university or college to support teaching, research and related activities and are provided in the form of a block grant. Institutions are free to distribute this grant internally at their own discretion, as long as the funds are used for the purposes for which they were provided.

There are two main elements to the block grant. Around 65% of the allocation of HEFCE block grants to higher education institutions is for teaching and reflects the numbers of students at each institution. The remainder is allocated to support research activities and is allocated selectively, on the basis of "quality" determined by the outcomes of the 1996 Research Assessment Exercise. These research block grants enable HEIs to act more effectively in winning 2nd and 3rd stream funding sources. Funds are also distributed to 73 further education colleges which provide higher education courses.

The five public and two private universities in the Catalonian region of Spain have entered into an agreement with the *Generalitat* (autonomous government) of Catalonia called the "Contract programme for improving university quality". Under the terms of this contract, the Catalonian administration establishes targets which the universities must meet in order to receive funds. The contract signifies a new relationship between the administration and the universities based upon collaboration and transparency. The Polytechnic University of Catalonia (UPC) was the first university to sign to the contract programme and reflects its special characteristics as a technical university at the service of society.

Governments are experimenting with new funding arrangements for HEIs to grant them more autonomy over their budgets. This financial devolution is an attempt to promote financial restructuring within HEIs to allow them to become more responsive to the problems they face in the external environment. Others experiments include tighter control and "earmarking" in which funds are not transferable around the institution.

The University of Twente devised a decentralised budgeting system in which each cost-centre (*e.g.* departments) received a lump-sum from the university and was given the autonomy to raise and spend money. In this context, each department has the responsibility to manage all three income streams. The University of Strathclyde also devolved the university budget to four faculty units and retained a strategic fund which was held centrally. Decentralisation can occur further in that research groups within departments can control their own funds.

The funding of Finnish universities has changed drastically since the 1980s. In particular, core government support has been reduced and earmarked which has led to the increasing importance of external, third stream funding sources. The University of Joensuu became a pilot institution under a scheme promoted by the Finnish government. This scheme allowed the university to experiment with a devolved lump-sum budgeting system wherein the university could spend its government allocation of money as it wished.

Stream 2: government research councils

In addition to government block-grant funding, HEIs also receive money from research councils. These are allocated on a competitive and largely national basis. As a result, funding from government research councils often do not require or reward a regional dimension in research activity.

Unlike most stream 1 funding, that from government research councils is, or at least is becoming, more "output" orientated, in that research funds are distributed in relation to performance criteria. Research councils are increasingly expecting greater engagement with the users and beneficiaries of research and insofar as this can involve regional partners, a regional dimension is creeping into this funding stream.

Stream 3: Income from all other sources

Many HEIs have responded to financial cuts in stream I funding sources by diversifying their funding base to include other sources. These other sources can be considered as third stream sources which comprise all other funds which HEIs receive outside government and their research councils. While this type of funding is extremely diverse in nature it generally includes a significant regional component. Typical elements are: income from endowments and investments; student fees; payment for services to industry; funds from local and regional government; profits from campus-based operations such as spin-off companies, patents and services; and catering and residential accommodations. The ability to develop third stream funding is heavily influenced by national and regional contexts and institutional histories.

Warwick University in Britain established an "earned income policy" to generate extra income. This policy is overseen by the Earned Income Group covering all the money generating from entrepreneurial activity at the university in over 50 profit earning units. The earned income approach allows the university to top-slice and cross-subsidise departments which do not work on a profit basis. The profits accrued from Warwick's entrepreneurial behaviour allowed it to employ 50 research fellows at a cost of £10 million. At Warwick University, there are now more university research centres (URC) than departments and core government support now only accounts for around one third of total financial support and stream 3 accounts for nearly half – a figure which has doubled over the last twenty years.

Increasingly, then, HEIs are acquiring funds from entrepreneurial activity and engagement with the external environment which is allowing them to diversify their funding base away from core government support. Most of this activity occurs in non-traditional units such as research centres, yet many mainstream academic departments, including those outside science and technology, are now also establishing such externally focused research centres, many of which are multi and transdisciplinary in nature, to tap into stream 2 and 3 funding sources.

Table 2 shows that in the case of several HEIs throughout Europe, additional third stream funding sources are approaching, or have overtaken, the level of core government money as a source of financial support. However, it must be noted that these examples represent institutions at the leading edge of securing third stream funds, and as a result, are rather atypical of the funding sources of most HEIs which are still reliant on public funds.

Table 3 highlights similar trends across the Australian university system.

Securing and sustaining third stream funding brings with it implications for the functioning of HEIs. For HEIs to seriously engage with the challenges they face in their environments and for them to fully exploit the opportunities which greater regional engagement offers, they need to adopt new forms of financial management. In particular, many HEIs are introducing new internal financial management

Table 2. **Sources of financial support at various HEIs, 1995**

Institution	Stream 1	Stream 2	Stream 3
University of Twente, Netherlands	76	3	21
University of Warwick, England	38	15	47
University of Joensuu, Finland	66	7	27
University of Chalmers, Sweden	55	25	18
University of Strathclyde, Scotland	45	4	51

Source: Clark (1998).

Table 3. **Income by source across the Australian university system**

Source	1989	1992	1994	1995
Commonwealth government grants	77.1	59.5	60.1	57.2
State government	4.6	4.5	1.9	1.4
Higher education councils	–	13.2	12.8	12.0
Fees and charges	5.9	10.4	10.8	11.7
Investment income, donations, bequests	8.5	5.4	2.9	5.1
Other sources	4.0	7.0	11.6	12.6
Total ($million)	4 274	5 962	6 833	7 536

Source: DEETYA selected higher education finance statistics.

techniques of budgetary devolution wherein departments and other basic units receive a lump-sum allocation which may meet only part of their costs.

Moreover, a key issue is the failure on the part of the universities to charge adequately for a contribution to their core infrastructure in relation to their externally funded activities. Universities need more realistic and accountable pricing of teaching and research services to ensure they have adequate surpluses which they can invest into the development of the institution and its regional contribution. There are also intra-institutional variations. For example, faculties such as science and medicine have more capacity to handle their own budgets. Moreover, financial devolution, while making departments more responsive, can set in centrifugal forces which can fracture HEIs. This can be prevented by a strong centre and institutional idea and through income redistribution where less profitable units are subsidised by more profitable ones to achieve a regional objective.

There are obvious consequences of a greater dependence on potentially volatile streams of funding in such areas as employment stability and the capacity of academics and institutions to make long-term commitments to research and infrastructure projects. What is equally clear is that stream 1 funding is no longer secure as governments attempt to reduce public expenditure and switch to new priorities. More significantly in research terms, it is often HEIs in metropolitan areas which are least dependent on stream 1 funding simply because of the strength of the local contribution to stream 3; this does not auger well for the role of universities in less favoured areas.

6

Teaching Management

Universities have always played a role as a source of, and repository for, knowledge. Access to this knowledge base has been achieved through the development of teaching. A core function of HEIs, then, has been to educate through the dissemination of its knowledge base. Whilst this teaching function was initially offered to a national elite, of politicians, industrialists, the clergy and civil servants, through the 20th century access has continually been widened to much larger groups. In spite of this extension of access, the development of the teaching function within long established HEIs has not been influenced by regional needs. Most recruit from, and provide graduates for, national and international markets.

However, the context for education provision is changing as a result of demands to create more regionally relevant education systems. Such demands are a result of policy changes from national governments, especially those associated with the concept of the "learning society", and from impulses within regions to enhance the relevance of the teaching function. Newer institutions and those incorporated into the higher education sector from outside are creating or have inherited a tradition of providing locally relevant education. For all types of HEIs, the challenge is to balance the need to meet regional labour needs with the need to encourage the national and global mobility and competitiveness of staff and students and to position the institution in the global market. In order to realise the potential of HEIs for regions, there is a requirement to bring together all regional education providers to reduce duplicative functions, enhance collaborative provision and create a regional learning system by expanding the overall size of the education market. However, this agenda is problematic as there are tendencies towards the localisation and delocalisation of teaching and learning as the regionally embedded HEI is renegotiated with the emergence of the virtual or placeless HEI. The following sections discuss management issues relating to several facets of the HEI-region teaching interface.

Student recruitment

- ◆ What is the institution's policy concerning regional recruitment?
- ◆ What mechanisms are in place to increase this?
- ◆ Is the institution involved in collaborative partnerships or quota arrangements with other regional HEIs to manage regional recruitment?

OECD 1999

HEIs face choices in terms of prioritising different student markets. Most HEIs operate, or would like to operate, in nationally and competitive student markets. In particular, larger comprehensive, urban universities are generally very competitive and over-subscribed and, as a result, are more selective and nationally/ internationally focused in terms of student recruitment. Moreover, subjects such as medicine function on a selection rather than a recruitment mode and therefore attach priority to attracting the best students with little regard to local recruitment. Further, distinctive or specialist subject areas often draw from national rather than regional student markets. Many HEIs then, would regard the attraction of the best students to the region from any source as a positive influence on regional development.

However, there are compelling arguments for making greater provision for more locally-based HE, not least because of the circumstances facing certain groups seeking higher education. For example, the steady shifting of costs in recent years away from the taxpayer and onto a full-time student's present or future family is a powerful reason why more full-time British students have each year chosen to go to a university close to their home (Robson, 1997). Further, most full- or part-time mature entrants (aged 25 and above on admission) are home-based and choose a local institution and most employed people seeking short courses or continuing professional development (CPD) activity prefer a relatively local supplier.

Many HEIs are distinctly local institutions, or have histories which connect them with the regional community and consequently have developed a strong role in educational provision for the region. In addition many national systems have regionally defined catchments for student recruitment.

> The Netherlands HE system is characterised by student recruitment areas. These are mainly regionally organised, with the majority of students choosing the closest university in geographical terms. The choice of the closest university is also stimulated by the fact that Dutch universities provide student housing only to a very limited extent, with students mainly living in the private housing sector. Altogether, this situation gives the Dutch universities a firm local rooting in terms of educational provision.

This emphasis on local recruitment is particularly evident in marginal and rural regions which suffer from under-provision.

> Universities in the peripheral regions of Scandinavian countries, such as Umeå, Sweden, Tromsø, Norway, Joensuu, Finland and Aalborg, Denmark, have a pro-active regional recruitment policy in an attempt to expand regional participation rates in post-compulsory education and to reduce the outflow of students from these peripheral areas to more populous areas, especially the national capitals.

There is an increasing need for HEIs to create regional educational opportunities. Many HEIs can make a positive contribution to enhancing the take-up of HE in the region by engaging with local schools and the FE sector. Further, it is essential that lagging regions retain the best students from the regional school system rather than losing them to other more prosperous regions.

> The North-East of England has the lowest participation rates in post-secondary school education amongst the regions of the United Kingdom. To increase the ability of local school children to reach university, a programme entitled "Students into Schools" has recently been established at Newcastle University working with the University of Northumbria at Newcastle with Training and Enterprise Council funding in which university students engage in mentor work in local schools to raise educational aspirations.

> The Regional Office at the University of Sheffield in Northern England has established the Early Outreach programme to raise educational aspirations in communities not participating in post-compulsory education. The programme involves 22 schools and over 1 000 children. The programme also works with parents to encourage them to help children realise their educational potential. The programme operates through mechanisms such as visits to the university, parents evenings, residentials and student tutoring and support.

HEIs can extend their student recruitment to adjacent regions which have been historically under-provided by HE.

> The formal unification between Hong Kong and mainland China in 1997 raises important questions concerning regional educational collaboration. When comparing Hong Kong with mainland China, the former has 0.5% of the total population but 2.5% of all university students (and 25% of all research students). Only a small proportion of students from China gain admission to Hong Kong's seven universities, a trend which is enhanced by bilingual course requirements and the cost of living in Hong Kong. The Open University in Hong Kong has entered into partnership with a provincial authority in China which offers courses at 7% of the fees charged in Hong Kong and translates material in Chinese.

Students and regional employment

- ◆ To what extent do HEIs recognise themselves as part of a regional educational supply chain?
- ◆ What mechanisms exist to create pathways between regional HEIs and regional firms, especially SMEs?
- ◆ To what extent is labour market information gathered to monitor the flow of graduates into the labour market?
- ◆ Does this process involve other regional stakeholders?

Graduate retention is an important mechanism through which a region can retain people with innovative, entrepreneurial and management capabilities. However, the levels of graduate retention in a region reflect an interplay of several different factors. These include: the ability of HEIs to provide courses and skills training which reflect the needs of the regional economy; the robustness, diversity and size of the regional economic base; the current state of the national economy; whether the student originates from the region; the type of higher education institution attended; and the socio-economic background of the student.

A recent report to the DfEE (1998a) by the University of Newcastle in England found that graduates with the worst employment record were those who study in their home region at "new" universities (the ex-polytechnics). These different levels of graduate unemployment display a strong regional dimension with local students graduating from "new" universities in the North-East of England having the worst unemployment figure outside London.

It is indisputable that HEIs are a major influence on the functioning of the regional labour market. When considering their relationship with employers in a regional context it is useful for HEIs to consider themselves as being located at the head of an "education supply chain" which produces educated people for the region. However, unlike a business enterprise situated in a similar supply chain position, HEIs devote relatively few resources to "marketing" their products (graduates) or to responding to signals about what the market wants.

This lack of marketing can be partly attributed to student funding regimes which reward "production" but not "sale" and the poorly developed mechanisms to undertake the marketing function outside careers services. If HEIs were in part rewarded for the delivery of graduates into employment, including local employment, they would clearly have an incentive to put more effort into marketing and economic development.

HEIs are confronted by a complex market place which consists of a variety of enterprises which currently, or might in the future, employ graduates. This diversity poses problems for HEIs in terms of understanding the variety of skills needs which have to be catered for. Three classes of enterprises can be identified. Firstly, the mature organisation (Type A) provides well established career routes and vocations for graduates, can choose to have relationships with selected universities and can influence the curriculum. Secondly, the rapidly developing company (Type B) will normally be inexperienced in graduate recruitment and there may not be the sectoral coherence of Type A organisations. As a result, they may be more difficult to reach by HEIs and they may well question whether HEIs are particularly focused on their needs. Student placements during degree programmes are likely to be an important mechanism for acquainting graduates with opportunities in this sector. Finally, the traditional small enterprise (Type C) employing less than 50 and probably less than 20, is unlikely to have mechanisms for selecting and screening graduates or to provide induction and this makes articulation of needs problematic. As a result, such companies generally do not want or cannot cope with "green" graduates and there may be the poorest coherence between traditional degree programmes and the skills/ knowledge which type C companies require.

Small firms with less than 250 employers account for the vast majority of firms in most national contexts. Increasing numbers of graduates are finding their way into such smaller firms via a number of routes such as pre-university placements, based learning and sandwich courses, vacation placements, part-time work, recruitment fairs, apprenticeships, teaching company programmes, recruitment at masters degree level and schemes for unemployed graduates.

Because of the great diversity of these small firms, it is very difficult to identify common needs. However, they generally require graduates to have acquired key transferable skills through their studies and work-based education, especially since SMEs do not have the resources, personnel and time to undertake skills training. Yet, it is unrealistic to expect HEIs to have the ability or knowledge to prepare graduates for the vast array of employment situations which they may encounter within SMEs. As a result, there is often a significant mismatch between the needs of SMEs and the skills of graduates; this can create much disillusionment amongst employers and employees.

A vast array of programmes have emerged to bridge the gap between the disparate worlds of HEIs and SMEs. Building partnerships and support mechanisms such as apprenticeship, matching and induction schemes, marketing and curriculum modification can ease the transition between the different institutional cultures and work practices. The challenge remains to develop an understanding of regional labour markets within such schemes.

In France, it is the DATAR (*Délégation à l'aménagement du territoire et à l'action régionale*) an autonomous central body in charge of regional development, through its ANTIDE *mission* (*Action nationale d'ingénierie du développement des territoires*), which pilots closer contacts between SMEs and higher education institutions. When partners are ready to collaborate, ANTIDE creates, on a defined territory, an industrial institute for innovation and development. These institutes put together all those interested in local development and favour close relationships between firms and educational institutions. The institute trains 20 young graduates per year with an associate degree or a university degree or a *grande école* diploma. Twenty per cent of the training time is devoted to development through interdisciplinary courses and the remaining 80% is devoted to a developmental project proposed by an SME. Such a scheme offers SMEs the possibility to concretise a project and students to enter SMEs in developmental position (accounting for 80% of students). Thirteen such institutes were planned to exist at the end of 1998 and it is expected that ANTIDE will create a total of 100 institutes in France by 2001.

Over the last two years, the Department for Education and Employment in Britain has funded nearly 30 projects concerned with the entry of graduates into the labour market. These projects focused upon how SMEs can make better use of new graduates within their organisations and how HE-business partnerships can be fostered. These projects brought together HE, employers and regional Training and Enterprise Councils.

OECD 1999

In 1991, the French authorities created new university professional institutes (IUP) recruiting students after a successful first or second university or equivalent year. A professional degree is delivered after a total of four university/higher education years. The aim of such institutes is to feed the local economy with highly competent professionals. Professionals are involved in curriculum development, in teaching and in final exams. The theoretical and practical teaching should generally be supplemented by a minimum of six months as intern in a firm. A key feature of many IUP degrees is that they are tailor-made according to student past experience. Both young students and adults co-exist in these courses.

HEIs face significant obstacles in terms of gathering information on the needs of firms within the regional labour market. Responsibility for monitoring regional employment opportunities for students is often uncoordinated and divided between academic departments, the student office, student's unions and careers services. Outside of the HEI a further obstacle is the lack of co-ordination of labour market information between various regional players such as other HEIs, employers, chambers of commerce and local and regional governments. Although there is a considerable supply of data on issues such as graduate employment and first destinations and employer needs, the means by which such information is collected and disseminated can differ radically between institutions. In this context, many regions would benefit from the establishment of a regional graduate Labour Market Information (LMI) system to systematically collect, process and disseminate information on the movement of graduates in the region.

In the case of East Finland, it is evident that the establishment of three regional universities has retained students and graduates in the region, especially in their areas of specialism – Joensuu (teacher training), Lappeenranta (engineering), Kuopio (medicine). However, the institutions recognise the need for better regional monitoring. Monitoring the progression of students into the labour market is divided between departments, the student office, student's unions and careers service. In Eastern Finland, the careers services are moving into a lead role and a joint database of new graduates from the three universities has been established.

The Department for Education and Employment (DfEE) in Britain has funded a range of activities within HEIs designed to enhance the employability of their students. The Higher Education Quality and Employability Division (HEQE) of the DfEE is funding 55 HE development projects at various HEIs over two years which cover several areas such as key skills; recording achievement; work experience; guidance for graduates; high level lifelong learning; labour market intelligence; graduate business start ups; innovation and creativity in the curriculum. These projects are intended to promote the development of higher education, to make it more responsive to the needs of the labour market and more effectively used by employers.

One problem faced by the University of Joensuu in Finland was that its curriculum was largely designed to meet the needs of large, often public sector, firms in the region. However, the recession and shrinkage of the public sector in Finland has led to a certain amount of labour immobility for recent graduates. As a result, the university has established the Entrepreneurial Education Programme to encourage students to develop a wider base of skills for the labour market. It is hoped that the programme will improve graduate retention and activity at the university's science park.

In France, in La Tronche, near Grenoble, the Research Centre for Health in the Army (CRSSA) favours transfers of technology through its association with an enterprise, a higher education and research institution and the Rhône-Alpes region. A contract is offered to a young graduate who is hosted by the CRSSA in co-operation with a higher education institution and is employed for a minimum of six months by a regional medium size firm. The Rhône-Alpes region subsidises a part of his/her salary while the firm benefits from the transfer of technology brought in by the young graduate.

There is a strong tendency within many countries for graduates to be pulled towards core economic regions and capital cities. In this sense, it is vital that HEIs in peripheral regions retain a fair share of the best school leavers and skilled graduates in the region otherwise they risk becoming net-importers of students and also net-exporters of graduates and as a result function as regionally disembedded educational providers.

Some particularly high levels of regional graduate retention are found amongst universities in Australia such as 56% at the University of Western Sydney, 80% amongst the three universities in Southern Australia and 65% at the University of Tasmania. Further, in the case of the University of Joensuu in Finland, 40% of students come from the local province and 70% from the region; subsequently, one third of graduates find employment in the province and one half in the region.

Localising the learning process

♦ Are there any courses which meet regional needs?
♦ What is the role of careers service in the process of localising learning?
♦ To what extent is postgraduate activity geared towards meeting regional needs?
♦ What mechanisms exist to monitor/accredit extra-curricular activities?
♦ How are students integrated in the region, in terms of course placements, accommodation, volunteering activities?

Higher education institutions can draw upon the specific characteristics of a region to aid learning and teaching. The creation of specialist locally-oriented courses which draw upon the characteristics of the region can give HEIs a competitive advantage in national and international student recruitment pools. Further, locally-oriented courses, especially those which are closely connected to growing industries in the region, can offer graduates greater chances of success and mobility in the regional labour market.

The Institute of Technology at Tralee in Western Ireland (one of eight such institutes established by the government) was established in 1977 to stimulate economic development in the rural Munster region. The university established courses which are directly linked to the human resource development needs of the economic development strategy being pursued by Munster.

Several universities in Australia have established regional-specific degree programmes. In particular, Deakin University in the State of Victoria in Australia has established courses at its rural campuses in areas such as natural resource management and agriculture and the University of Hawkesbury has sought to ensure that its teaching and research profile reflects the region's needs in areas such as agriculture and tourism. Further, a number of links have been established between research expertise at La Trobe University and regional agricultural and environmental research bodies.

The Faculty of Education at the University of Joensuu in Eastern Finland accounts for over two-thirds of activity at the university. The university also runs the Teacher Education Department in an outreach campus at Savonlinna. This teaching role of the university has dramatically increased the educational level of teachers in Eastern Finland. The Faculty of Education is also developing postgraduate education and runs programmes for the regional polytechnic. The faculty runs the Research and Development Centre for IT in Education which involves local schools and businesses. This centre is involved in an EU programme to develop the region's IT infrastructure, especially in relation to rural areas.

The University of South Australia, in conjunction with the Australian Centre for Automotive Management, has developed a number of graduate programmes to meet the needs of the regional motor vehicle manufacturing and distribution industry. Further, the University of Tasmania has identified a number of themes for teaching which are of significance to the state which include Antarctic Ocean studies and wilderness studies.

HEIs can act as a resource for certain sectors of the regional economy by offering undergraduate training which will provide a supply of graduates for the labour market.

The Swinburne University of Technology in Melbourne established a regional campus in an area which is heavily dependent upon the tourism industries. However, concern existed within the local community regarding the lack of appropriate tertiary education in tourism studies. The regional campus was approached by two local tourism boards which raised the need for a tourism degree. A first degree in Tourism and Enterprise Management was developed drawing upon expertise from the tourism industry, the university, local government and industry, who now form the advisory board for the degree.

Florida Atlantic University in the United States interfaces traditional academic courses to the general community through outreach programmes. These include co-operative education programmes based around work experience; 2+2 programmes between the community colleges and the university to allow ease of transition; the 60+ audit programme which, under state law offers those over 60 years the ability to audit credit courses free of cost; and finally, the College Reach-Out programme in which all ten state universities encourage participation in post-secondary education amongst disadvantaged social groups.

The University of Kuopio in Eastern Finland was initially established as an institution specialising in health and medicine. As a result of this focus, around half of the university's graduates find employment in the fields of social and health care. Moreover, the university makes a significant contribution to the region's health infrastructure, especially in areas such as nursing and social service provision. This is of particular importance considering that morbidity and mortality rates in Eastern Finland are above national average.

Locally-based teaching is also an effective way of exposing the region to the work of HEIs and the skills and talents of its students.

The University of Edinburgh in Scotland offers music students the opportunity to pursue an option entitled Music in the Community. The course collaborates with local professional performing orchestras as well as the health, social and prison services where students are involved in creative arts therapy. Students undertake community placements which are credit bearing. The benefits of this type of community-based teaching are manifold: students learn a number of transferable skills during hands-on community work and as a result may increase their performance in the local musical labour market, and various groups in the community, many of which have no previous contact with the university, are exposed to its work.

Postgraduate activity also embeds the teaching activities of HEIs in the region. The postgraduate community is often involved in high-level research activity which can be of benefit to the region. Higher degree university research, then, can be an effective tool of technology transfer to the region and a way of embedding highly skilled graduates in the regional economy. HEIs can also draw upon representatives from local industry to add practical experience to the teaching process through the status of external associate professors.

The graduate entrepreneurial programme at the University of Adelaide offers opportunities for recent graduates to move from the university into business using skills acquired at university. Graduates with entrepreneurial ideas are offered access to a range of supporting mechanisms such as courses, supervision and venture capital. Sixteen businesses involving graduates have been supported in this way.

Various mechanisms have been established within HEIs to promote the regional relevance of the student learning experience. In particular, project work can be undertaken collaboratively with regional partners and can be focused upon regional issues.

The University of Aalborg in North Jutland, Denmark, has developed a problem-oriented, project-organised educational system which was developed to ensure a dialectic relationship between academic theory and professional practice. This system, the "Aalborg Experiment", engages with local companies to concretise and analyse problems. The student's educational process becomes an instrument of technology and knowledge transfer to the region and students completing such project oriented work have showed improved performance in the local labour market. The university is also developing Ph.D. industrial programmes through which a study plan is prepared with a company which also pays a proportion of course expenses.

In Britain, Teaching Company Schemes (TCS) have been established to transfer university expertise to local industry. Researchers work in firms and help in problem solving while being registered as postgraduates with the university. TCSs are co-ordinated regionally, and at the five universities in the North-East of England, there are over 30 TCS in operation working with firms such as British Steel and ICI. The presence of regional TCS consultants with a brief to act as brokers in putting together Teaching Company programmes has been instrumental in bringing together HEIs and companies that might not otherwise have worked together.

The Regional Office at the University of Sheffield in Northern England co-ordinates the PLUS scheme (Project Link University of Sheffield). This scheme builds upon project work undertaken by final year and postgraduate students and aims to bring together students and external organisations to conduct projects. Over 2 000 students across 43 departments have taken part in the scheme and a director has been appointed to outline opportunities and establish codes of practice. The PLUS scheme is supported by several Training and Enterprise Councils (TECs) in neighbouring regions and is an important trust and information building exercise between the university and region.

HEIs, then, can localise their learning process, by drawing upon the region as a resource for teaching and by embedding the work of undergraduate and postgraduate students in the region. However, overly localised teaching programmes can have several shortcomings. Firstly, if tied too closely to the economic base of the region, courses can be susceptible to cycles of growth and contraction in the regional economy. Further, regionally-oriented courses may have a limited appeal in terms of attracting non-local students and could also adversely affect the performance of students in national labour markets. Moreover, many HEIs regard their role as generating expert knowledge and providing graduates of the highest quality. As a result, meeting the more practical needs of the region is an option not taken by many HEIs.

One cannot assume that young people in (or outwith) a region will be attracted to study those courses which are particularly in the region's economic interests. Indeed, there is evidence that in areas of economic hardship, home-based students will see a degree as a way of escaping from the region and will explicitly reject area. There is a real tension here. HEIs have always enabled young people to leave their home region in search of the kinds of jobs they want elsewhere, as well as being a means of matching the acquisition of knowledge and skills to the region's developing economy. Moreover, many HEIs find it difficult to be responsive to the needs of the regional economy due to the significant time-lags between developing a degree course. HEIs, then, have to seriously consider the problems associated with localising the curriculum.

Promoting lifelong learning, continuing professional development and training

♦ How is continuing education and continuing professional cevelopment activity organised – separately or departmentally?
♦ Have external or independent enterprises been established within HEIs to extend professional education provision to the region?
♦ Is such provision undertaken in collaboration with other regional stakeholders?
♦ Which regional partners are involved in meeting regional training needs?
♦ Should HEIs be involved in a production culture (selling what you make) or a market culture (making what you can sell)?

HEIs are increasingly playing a regional role in meeting professional and vocational educational demand in the labour market. Technological change means that skills acquired are soon rendered obsolete and career progression is no longer linear. The implication is that there is a significant increase in the demand for adult and continuing education and a greater emphasis on lifelong learning, and on the critical role of skills development in maintaining and increasing national competitiveness. As a result of such changes, there have been many efforts to ensure that HE provision more closely matches what are seen to be local, regional and national skills needs.

Major initiatives have been introduced in France to enhance the status of vocational education alongside the well established higher education sector. In particular, in the 1980s, short-cycle vocational educational courses were introduced (BEP and CAP studied in vocational lycées) as well as the "vocational baccalauréat" which benefited from the strong symbolism associated with the baccalauréat qualification. It was seen as essential to integrate these qualifications with the business sector which should take a responsibility in promoting work place-based, vocational education. In this sense, vocational experience within university courses have been introduced to reduce the time between the completion of studies and obtaining a job.

In addition to undergraduate and postgraduate degree programmes, HEIs are diversifying their teaching activities to meet the growing continuing professional development (CPD), continuing education (CE) and training needs of the region. This can take many forms such as adult liberal education and tailored and specialist continuing professional development courses for regional organisations, often undertaken in partnership with other local bodies.

However, in the absence of lead agencies to articulate the skills needs of the region, it is often difficult for HEIs to organise suitable provision. As a result, it is often unclear as to the extent to which professional and business training provision from HEIs is genuinely demand-driven or simply draws upon the existing strengths and interests within HEIs. The ability to respond to regional skills needs is a particular problem when engaging with smaller organisations whose requirements are less clearly organised and articulated. This problem of market responsiveness is being counteracted through the establishment of units to provide professional education. These can exist within established centres for CE and/or CPD or through the creation of separate and often independently-run business schools. Often working in collaboration with other education providers and regional partners, such schools are meeting the growing demand for professional and business training courses in the region.

The Twente Business School (TBS) in Eastern Netherlands, a private institution, is a co-operative venture between the three universities of Twente, Groningen and Eindhoven and draws upon staff from other local educational institutions and firms.

At Lappeenranta University of Technology in Finland, the School of Business Administration was established with substantial financial support from the city and a local foundation, the Vyborg Economic Society. This local involvement was prompted as the city and the university had a common aim of increasing the level of business education and training to aid the development of the area.

Southern Cross University in Australia has forged a reputation for co-operative education and training programmes in full partnership with employers to specifically meet the needs of the workplace. The university has established centres for professional development (CPDs) which identifie needs amongst practitioners which are then addressed by professionals who oversee the production of learning materials. Through the CPDs, the university provides tailor made courses for several industrial groups many of which are delivered through distance learning and work place study groups. Further, at Deakin University in Australia "Deakin Australia" has been established to design and deliver accredited and non-accredited tailored training courses to a range of private and public sector enterprises.

However, whilst many HEIs have embraced the rhetoric of lifelong learning, few have concretised it through mechanisms such as regional credit transfer between institutions. This is particularly true of more competitive universities in prosperous regions.

Changing forms of educational provision

♦ What mechanisms exist for promoting flexible education provision such as satellite campuses, accreditation networks, on-line courses and outreach centres?
♦ How do HEIs maintain institutional coherence in the light of this multi-territorial educational provision?
♦ Are regional HEIs drawing upon new forms of ICT-based course delivery to enhance educational opportunities to a wider group?
♦ What are the tensions between place-based and virtual forms of education provision?
♦ What mechanisms are in place to increase access to learners in the region who have been traditionally under-represented in higher education?

Increasing access and providing flexible learning

HEIs are moving away from traditional forms of course delivery and the standard three-year bachelor degree in order to provide flexible packages of higher education to a variety of audiences. Most HEIs have extended their teaching activities to offer access to HE for traditionally under-represented groups and are experimenting with new forms of course delivery especially to those located in rural or marginal areas hitherto poorly served by higher education.

The development and provision of tailored access courses are effective mechanisms which offer non-traditional students routes into HEIs. However, many older universities are often reticent to recognise, and take-up candidates from, such alternative learning routes. A particular challenge facing HEIs is to establish mechanisms for accrediting learning routes between university and non-university institutions on a regional basis.

Educational institutions in the North-East of England have developed several access mechanisms. The Tees Region Open College Network (TROCN) chaired by Teesside University, and the Wearside and Durham Open College Network are authorised validating agencies (AVA) for access courses which also link up with the Tyneside Open College Federation (TOCF) and UNILINK based at Northumbria University to create a network for access provision which spans the region. These networks involve over 30 colleges and all the regional universities.

Although most HEIs are located in areas of population concentration, they can offer education access, through distance learning and outreach centres, to people in remote and rural areas. This can be an important integrating tool in sparsely populated areas where HEIs are used as part of wider welfare state programmes to increase service provision to marginal and remote areas.

The University of Umeå was established in the 1960s in Norrland, the northern region of Sweden which has low population density. The university was originally established to facilitate access to higher education in the region, especially in relation to providing qualified public sector personnel and to contribute to the development of the culture of Norrland. To fulfil its educational role, the university has developed an active programme of distance learning through the establishment of "distributed courses" in remote towns throughout Norrland.

In most communes throughout Northern Sweden there are higher education study centres, often attached to local schools, but it has not proved cost-effective to run a complete university course at such a centre. Through a grouping of study centres it has, however, now been possible to offer selected courses at three or four places at the same time, whereby a sufficient number of participants can be attracted to each course so that it can be run without loss for the university departments concerned. The centres are organised jointly by the University of Umeå local government and industry. However, course funding at Swedish universities is based upon performance (*i.e.* outputs). As a result, high drop-out rates at some regional centres have undermined the stability of some distributed courses.

The University of Turku in Finland established the Archipelago Development Project to aid the development of the fishing and aquaculture industries in the numerous inhabited islands and coastal areas around Turku. The project was established in the light of the need to halt the population decline and economic decay of the area. It is co-ordinated through the Centre for Extension Studies at the university and is run through a multi-field management group which includes the island municipalities and local government. The project provides training and field courses for local industries but also the development of new skills through a telework project. The project drew upon several central government and local funding sources and also acted as a vehicle for links to be established with neighbouring countries such as Estonia.

The Hong Kong Baptist University (HKBU) reflects Hong Kong's position as a region with multiple territorial allegiances. HKBU has established a campus in Beijing as part of the University of Tsinghua with funds from a Hong Kong philanthropist. The campus exists to extend educational opportunities to mainland China and provides exchange courses and summer schools for staff and students. Further HKBU leads a consortium of universities entitled the David C. Lam Institute, comprising several Chinese universities and others in Asia and Europe. The aim of the institute is to provide better understanding of East-West relations.

In France, "university antennas" have been created in response to the growing social demand for higher education. University antennas are administratively dependent upon a mother university and are largely supported by the local government in which it is located. Staff are assigned to the antennas who largely conduct short first year university courses. Most students attending antennas are from lower socio-economic backgrounds and much attention is focused towards ensuring that such students progress to full university courses at the mother university. Antennas are a component of regional higher education growth poles centred around the mother university.

Higher education provision is also offered through open education which offers flexible and non-placed learning and access to groups from non-traditional backgrounds. Differences in national systems exist in terms of the organisation of open university education. In some national contexts open education is organised through a separate institution, whereas in others it is mediated through individual universities. Open education can reach large numbers of people throughout the region by utilising information and communication technologies (ICTs). However, much distance and open education usually draws upon traditional forms of course delivery such as televisual aides and course books rather than advanced technological infrastructures.

The Open University (OU) in Britain, established in 1969, is regarded as the pioneer of modern distance education at university level. The student body includes over 200 000 people, including over 20 000 from overseas which makes it the largest university in the British system. A range of distance learning techniques are used such as e-mail and web courses, but TV and radio programme courses remain the most used tools. These are supported by a tutorial system. The OU is organised through a central headquarters near London and centres in every region of the British Isles. The OU is able to deliver the most cost-effective education in Britain, and as a result has been the major beneficiary of government grant increases.

Southern Cross University in Australia has established three Open Learning Access Centres (OLAC) which are affiliated agencies for Open Learning Australia. Advisory boards at these centres include regional community representatives. The centres have recently won an award for the provision of facilities to deaf students and have been investigated by those wishing to replicate similar models of flexible learning provision.

The virtual university

As a consequence of technological developments and a wide range of social and economic transformations, a number of significant changes are occurring in the nature and role of higher education provision. In particular, developments in telecommunication networks (such as broadcasting, cable, Internet, World Wide Web) are challenging the role of the place-based university in the creation, preservation and transmission of knowledge. Developments in ICTs enable a whole host of actors, including HEIs and other public and private institutions – individually or in partnership – to mould, and respond to, educational needs in radical ways. Thus, the monopolistic position of many HEIs in a regional and national context is being supplanted by external education providers who can enter the regional learning system and offer courses via mediums such as the Internet. HEIs are responding to such threats by offering web-based courses around the globe, creating a patchwork of internal and external HE provision in regions delivered by a range of actors.

> The University of Phoenix in the United States exemplifies expanding education provision outwith its own region to cover the whole country. The university now has 48 000 degree-credit students who are distributed in 57 learning centres across 12 states and has prospered from exploiting niche programmes, especially in IT and business.
> Western Governors University was founded by the governors of 18 western states in the United States and corporate partners including Apple, Microsoft and IBM with a vision of making higher education more accessible through distance education. The governors recognised that the well-being of their states and the nation depends heavily on a postsecondary education system that responds to the needs of a changing economy and society. They realised that their dwindling state budgets and growing student populations were making their ability to respond increasingly difficult. This "virtual university" delivers education packages through ICTs and conventional correspondence methods and a network of local centres backed by corporate sponsors.

The changing nature of educational provision and institutional forms based upon the introduction of ICTs has been associated with the concept of the "virtual university" which suggests that the role and remit of HEIs are in a period of complex re-negotiation. The emergence of this place-less institution can be ascribed to several developments. First, the availability of technological advanced infrastructures. Second, the move to mass higher education provision which requires significant developments in teaching practices. Third, the Internet represents a changing context of knowledge production in which the status and authority of formal place-based teaching is altered, and to some extent, undermined. Together such developments can represent a disembedding of HEIs from particular places and communities.

In response to the challenge many HEIs are experimenting with types of HE delivery which move away from place-bound teaching and traditional academic terms.

Southern Cross University in Australia (SCU) was established in 1994 and had its origins in a small teachers college. It has a novel institutional form in that its name is not directly associated with a locality. This lack of geographical ties reflects its commitment to distance learning. 9 000 students are enrolled over eight campuses with 40% studying at a distance throughout every state in Australia and overseas. SCU also offers courses in South-East Asia and around the globe and through the web.

The University of the Highlands and Islands Project aims to establish a collegiate federal university in the rural and remote highlands and islands region of northern Scotland by the year 2001. The project aims to establish 13 campuses in a region which has a population of one third of a million people but is not currently served by a university. The proposed university will draw heavily upon the use of new technologies to create integrated services over the campus network.

In the Catalonian region of Spain, most universities have created separated branches to flexibly respond to the requirements of the continuing education market. Through the creation of foundations, universities extend their coverage over the Catalan territory. In particular, the Open University of Catalonia was created in 1995 to respond to the demands of a highly skilled workforce which were not being met by traditional university education in the region. The university operates via a virtual campus which covers the whole of Catalonia by means of a computer network. Students and professors connect daily to the virtual campus, which provides full access to a vast range of university facilities such as on-line multimedia and interactive educational materials, tutorial support, library resources or administrative services.
The Open University of Catalonia has set up a territorial development plan which involves a network of student support centres guided by a head office in Barcelona. These support centres not only cover the needs of university students, in terms of computer access and multimedia and library resources, but they also fulfil a very important role as university extension poles, offering the local community a doorway to higher education and providing opportunities to those with no previous qualifications.

In essence, developments associated with the virtual university represent a "headquarter-branch plant" model of HEI decentralisation which is used to create economies of scale and reduce unit costs within education provision. An "education industry" is flourishing around virtual, flexible and distance education provision backed by corporate sponsors and major IT and telecommunication firms whose logic is inherently transnational. This represents a significant threat to the regional HEI as their own involvement in flexible education provision is being undermined by new players, and students consider the benefits of the fast growing alternatives.

Extending participation

The expansion of HEIs and the growth of mass higher education provision in many countries have resulted in the extension of educational opportunities to groups traditionally under-represented in higher education, such as ethnic minorities, returning and adult learners, or those with disabilities. Further, in many national contexts, HE provision is being tailored to meet the specific requirements of indigenous groups and ethnic minority/cultural groups.

> Several universities in Australia are actively engaged in increasing educational provision to Aboriginal and Torres Strait islander communities, Australia's original inhabitants. The University of New South Wales is improving access to the university for members of these groups. Moreover, Southern Cross University has established the College of Indigenous Australian Peoples and the Gungil Jindibah Support Centre, predominantly staffed by Aboriginal and Torres Strait islander people, to increase university participation amongst these indigenous groups.

HEIs also have to respond to the changing characteristics of the regional population, in terms of, for example, demographic profile, social and ethnic structure, and develop course provision which reflects such changes.

> The South Florida region in the United States has experienced a four-fold increase in population since the 1960s which has placed tremendous growth pressures upon the regional educational system. The universities in the region have attempted to meet the demands in a number of ways. For example, Florida Atlantic University has established distinctive programmes to serve the needs of the over-60s population. Such courses have attracted an audience of over 12 000 students and reflect the response of the university to the needs of the large, wealthy and rapidly expanding retirement communities in South Florida.

HEIs are also deploying strategies such as mergers and establishing distance learning centres in other regions to expand student intake. For example, many HEIs are establishing campuses in centres of population concentration within the region to access a wider student market. This is one way in which HEIs can enter new student markets, such as the overseas student population.

A recent survey of Australian universities (Garlick, 1998) revealed the extent to which most universities in the country have established associated campuses to extend educational opportunities, especially to non-metropolitan areas. For example, La Trobe University has established seven rural campuses which have brought higher education to a group which was denied access because of its physical isolation.

Further, Massey University, in Palmerston North, New Zealand, has expanded away from its region to other parts of the country. This growth in satellite campuses has enabled the university to consolidate its activity in its main campus in Palmerston North. Southern Cross University has also established university centres in Brisbane and Sydney to enter the educational market in these two large conurbations.

Many older universities also have a significant history as providers of non-award bearing liberal adult education. Such provision takes the form of evening classes or short courses which are undertaken for a variety of motives ranging from pleasure or interest to more structured vocational skills. Older universities, as part of their civic role, have often developed an extensive range of liberal adult courses with large regional audiences, many of which are undertaken in small regional centres such as village halls.

The University of Bristol in South-West England has a long tradition of educational outreach and the provision of liberal adult education which dates back to the nineteenth century when university staff would run classes in rural towns in the region. Today, the university is the main provider of adult and continuing education in the region and provides eight tutors who work across the region. There are over 15 000 enrolments on non-credit bearing continuing education courses which are undertaken throughout the region in a number of educational institutions and also libraries, village halls and churches.

Enhancing the regional learning system

◆ To what extent is there a coherent vision of an education system existing at the regional level? Do HEIs acknowledge the need to develop education on a regional basis?
◆ Are procedures in place to support regional collaboration between HEIs?
◆ Is there a credit transfer system between education institutions and what links exist between the university and non-university higher education sector?
◆ Is the regional agenda incorporated into institutional human resources policies?
◆ Do HEIs monitor graduate output into the regional labour market?

One of the most important challenges facing HEIs is to create a coherent system, in which regional stakeholders work together to develop the overall capacity of human resources in the region. The potential for developing such regional learning systems varies significantly between countries. For example, some countries have a long history of regional co-operation between education providers, whilst other national systems are characterised by lack of regional coherence.

In spite of the growing interest in the concept of the learning society and learning region, there are few examples outside of the United States of systematic regional co-operation between different segments of the educational system, such as schools, universities and other higher education institutions, and even fewer examples which demonstrate an awareness of the link between education provision and economic development at a regional level. At best, many HEIs display a reactive approach to engagement in regional development and regional human resources management.

One of the key aspects of growing the regional learning system is to encourage communication and co-operation between the various educational providers (university and non-university higher education institutions, further education (FE) institutions and schools) and the various organisations involved in local regional economic development. All HEIs in a region have an interest in raising the overall levels of educational participation. "Growing the market" as opposed to mercantilism and market-share protection strategies can avoid duplication and financial wastage and enhance regional economic development.

Unfortunately, many regions are characterised by market specialisation and fragmentation amongst FE and HE providers. There is evidence to suggest that HEIs are reluctant to enter into formal arrangements with FE providers as they are unsure of "quality" issues, and in particular the ability of students to undertake HE courses. There is also reluctance to establish a national system which links FEIs and HEIs on a regional basis as this has the potential disadvantage of blurring the distinctive missions of institutions within the two sectors. For example, many of the needs in the national labour market for intermediate and vocational skills are met by the distinctive nature of the FE sector. This distinctiveness could be eroded if the FE sector focused upon courses which trained people for entry into the HE system. Moreover, HEIs which attempt to strategically reposition themselves to enter other teaching markets in the regional higher education system, by providing access and foundation courses and aiming at non-traditional courses, may encounter competition with other regional educational providers who currently focus on such activities.

In Britain, in spite of the establishment of a unified system of higher education in 1992, there is little evidence of co-operation at a regional level between the new universities (former polytechnics) and other universities. Similarly, there are few links between universities and FE colleges and little recognition of them as "strategic partners" within the regional economic development process.

However, the further education (FE) sector in Britain plays a significant role in developing the links between education provision and local and regional economic development. Yet, the potential of FE is hampered by a limited recognition of its role within regional regeneration by other agencies. The growth of a learning system at the regional level, then, suffers from a fragmentation and multiplicity of agencies involved in regional economic development and a lack of regional and sub-regional co-ordination between colleges.

Examples of well co-ordinated educational systems which bring together different educational providers do exist. Of particular importance to the construction and credibility of such a system is the flexibility of routes between different institutions for students.

The higher education system of South Florida in the United States is characterised by co-operation which is a result of external forces and also the desire to meet the demands of the fast growing population in the region. Co-operation exists between the community colleges and state universities in that they work together to provide educational programmes which can lead students from college courses to bachelor degrees. Moreover, the Board of Regents who oversee activities within all the universities in the state, established mechanisms to ensure that there was no duplication amongst graduate programmes at two of the universities in the southern part of the state, Florida Atlantic University and Florida International University. The is also evidence of co-operation between public and private universities in the state, especially in terms of participation in state wide research institutes such as the Florida Centre for Environmental Studies.

The original legislature of Southern Cross University in Australia required that it became a partner with the New South Wales TAFE and the New South Wales Department of School Education in the development of a shared educational campus at Coffs Harbour. This collaborative cross-sector project is the first of its kind in Australia. Collaboration ensures flexible pathways between the partner institutions, especially through joint degree programmes.

In Finland, regional co-operation between the recently established non-university higher education institutions (AMKs) and the universities is one of the challenges for the future. Funding and management decisions within the AMK institutions are based upon local and regional issues and as a result their regional remits are much stronger than the regional universities in Eastern Finland. However, the universities also have a regional remit and so come into competition with the AMK institutions for resources and students. There are a number of differences between the two sectors. For example, budget funding for the universities is based upon performance (i.e. number of outputs) whilst for the AMK institutions it is based upon enrolments (i.e. number of inputs). It has been suggested that the funding of the entire higher educational system be placed on a performance based system. There is also co-operation between the two sectors. In particular, the University of Joensuu, as the largest teacher training institute in the region plays a significant role in the training of AMK teachers.

In Australia, the Nirimba Education Precinct was established as a joint venture between the University of Western Sydney, Western Sydney Institute of TAFE and the state and catholic education systems to deliver lifelong learning opportunities and training programmes for residents and business in the Western Sydney area.

Such co-operative arrangements can not only cover whole regions, but can cross national and regional boundaries.

> The University of Vaasa, Finland, and the University of Umeå, Sweden, are located adjacent to each other across the Gulf of Bothia, an area characterised by a long history of co-operation. The two universities have developed several collaborative initiatives to aid the regional development process in this wider cross border gulf region. These include the development of joint education programmes for young teachers and researchers in Eastern Europe, co-operation with a large firm to develop management training programmes, and enterprise programmes to encourage entrepreneurship in Finland and Sweden.

There are also several examples of mergers and alliances between regional educational institutions which have the added benefit of securing expansion and co-operation without incurring the investment costs of new developments.

> Many of the newer universities in Britain (the former polytechnics) have expanded through mergers with local teaching colleges and, as a result, have developed a large teaching function. For example Strathclyde University merged with Jordanhill College to make it the largest centre for teacher training in the United Kingdom and the University of the West of England in the South West of England incorporated two regional health colleges to expand its existing Faculty of Health and Social Care.

An important aspect of the regional learning system is the role of students within the region. Students, and graduates who are retained in the region, are an important asset to a region in terms of their capacity to sustain certain forms of economic, social and cultural activities.

> At many state universities in the United States there is a strong perception of students as future leaders of the state. This is partly derived from the high percentage of students staying in-state to study at most public universities in the United States because of the cheaper in-state tuition fees. Nevertheless, a strong university-student-state identity exists at most public universities in the United States and students are regarded as the life-blood of the region.

7

Research Management

Research within HEIs, especially the university sector, has traditionally focused on the generation of "basic" knowledge for the national/international academic community and avoided the application of established knowledge for the local/ regional community. Some researchers in HEIs have been reluctant to seek external research sponsors and have often been guarded towards collaborative research activities. Furthermore, many national funding regimes exacerbate inter-institutional competition rather than collaboration in terms of research activity and funding.

However, there are a number of trends which are encouraging partnership and regionalisation within higher education research, not least the emergence of alternative, often local, sources of funding and conditions from many funders who require research to be conducted on a collaborative basis. At the same time it must be noted that the logic of research collaboration within HEIs is as much international/ national as regional/local. The following sections highlight a number of trends relevant to the regional management of research such as the changing nature of the research enterprise, the use of the region as a source of research and various interfaces which have been developed for promoting the technology transfer process.

The changing nature of research and knowledge production

It is important to understand the ways in which the production of knowledge is being reconfiguring and how this is altering the conduct of research within HEIs. It has been observed that over the last decade there has been a shift in the way in which knowledge is produced and disseminated. This has been described as a shift from Mode 1 to Mode 2 knowledge production (Gibbons *et al.*, 1994). According to this thesis, Mode 1 knowledge is homogeneous, disciplinary and hierarchical and reflects the way in which knowledge has been traditionally produced in autonomous and distinct academic disciplines. Mode 2 knowledge is heterarchical, transient, transdisciplinary, socially accountable and reflexive and undertaken in a context of application. The emergence of transdisciplinary research centres within HEIs which engage with external research partners and increasingly rely on third stream funding sources can be situated within this new mode of knowledge production.

In this new context, HEIs no longer have a monopoly on knowledge production and must enter into strategic alliances with a range of knowledge producers in order to remain at the cutting edge of research. HEIs, then, are increasingly seeking external research partners to tap into wider knowledge networks and meet the rising costs of research. This is being achieved by expansion of research activities away from traditional academic units to new collaborative units such as research centres and science parks. The important point for HEIs is that these new vehicles for knowledge production have significant organisational implications. In particular, research centres often have an explicit regional *raison d'être* and function on a multi-disciplinary and collaborative basis. The expansion of such centres is also a strategy from HEIs to compete with the growing number of private research institutes. In this new context of knowledge production, HEIs can become involved in the co-creation, co-ownership and co-use of research knowledge with the partners who cohabit the learning region (Duke, 1998).

Regionally based research

♦ To what extent do HEIs draw upon the characteristics of the region to develop research activity?
♦ What other regional partners are drawn into this process?
♦ How have such research links established?
♦ What mechanisms exist to reward and acknowledge research which is regionally-based outside of peer review processes such as academic journals?

Historically, the faculty mix of HEIs often reflected the physical, socio-economic and cultural characteristics of the region. HEIs have responded to opportunities provided by the regional context by developing research agendas which reflect these characteristics. The region is often used as a test bed/laboratory for research which gives them a competitive advantage both nationally and internationally. A key question to pursue is the extent to which research is driven by the characteristics of the region and what new and developing opportunities exist for regionally relevant research.

Many HEIs draw upon the characteristics of the natural environment, history and cultural traditions of the region to generate research which can provide national and international lessons.

Forestry is one of the largest natural assets and economic sectors of Finland and the University of Joensuu in Eastern Finland has developed a strong research profile from this asset. The university has been able to accrue large sums of research income from central government and regional income sources for research into forestry and has been able to compete successfully with other centres in Finland and attract one of the twelve nationally designated centres of research excellence. The university's Faculty of Forestry is complemented by the European Forest Institute, the Finnish Forestry Research Institute, the Joensuu Forest Research Station and has established links with the Institute of Forestry and Wood Technology at the regional polytechnic. The university's connection with forestry, then, has enabled it to raise its research profile, promote the economic development of the region and the local forest industry and acted as a catalyst to forge links with other regional institutions involved in forestry.

The South Florida region in the United States provides a rich focus for academic research. The Ocean Engineering programme and the Hurricane Centre at Florida Atlantic University and the Rosentiel School at the University of Miami are internationally recognised centres in tropical environments. Further, the Florida Centre for Environmental Studies was established by the Regents of the State University System of Florida to synthesise and communicate knowledge on the Florida ecosystem and other similar ecosystems world-wide.

University of Joensuu established the Karelian Research Institute to carry out research into the history, culture and ecology of border regions such as Karelia. This new research centre was important for the university in a number of respects. Firstly, it was a way for the university to expand into a multifaculty away from its narrow base as a teacher training institute and hence contribute more broadly to regional economic development. Secondly, it was a mechanism which would promote local cultural development, especially in terms of raising the national and international profile of the region. Further, a group of students were also involved in compiling a multi-media package to depict certain aspects of Karelian culture.

Research activities at HEIs can be directed towards promoting the growth of regionally-based industrial clusters, or in some cases, aiding the establishment and development of new clusters of economic activity.

Southern Cross University in the Gold Coast region of Australia, is involved in the development of the region's tea tree oil industry in connection with the Main Camp tea tree oil group. As a result of this activity, the Australian Tea Tree Oil Research Institute (ATTORI) has been established. Funding for this venture came from offering research shares on expected market results of the research. The success of this venue has stimulated research activities into a number of other natural remedy products through a new research company, the Australian Agriculture Institute and has led to interest in a technology park for natural products.

The University of Newcastle in the North of England is collaborating in the development of the International Centre for Life which aims to link research at the university to the region's bio-genetics industry. The centre comprises a BioScience wing, providing specialist space from SMEs in biotechnology and the Genetics Institute, which is led by the university's Department of Human Genetics to conduct research into inherited diseases. The centre is being jointly funded by national and European money. It is intended that the centre will be used to establish the city of Newcastle as one of the world's leading centres for genetic research.

In common with many Baltic countries, Lithuania is heavily dependent upon the maritime industries and forms a strategic water transport corridor between Eastern and Western Europe. The University of Klaipeda in Lithuania, plays a central role in the country's maritime industry. This role has been enhanced with the relocation of much maritime activity to Lithuania in 1990 in the wake of independence from the former Soviet Union. In 1997, the Maritime Institute and the Maritime Technical Faculty were established at the university to provide training and education for the sector. The university is involved in several collaborative projects with neighbouring countries also dependent upon maritime industries such as Latvia, Germany and the Netherlands.

The University of Lappeenranta in Eastern Finland has established "Metalnet" to help local SMEs working in the metal industry. This activity is co-ordinated through the Centre for Training and Development at the university and the Centre of Excellence in High Technology Metal Constructions. Seventy regional firms participate in this project.

The University of Midsweden in Sweden's northern inland region has established the Tourism Research Centre with financial support from the European Union's "Objective 6" regional funding, national government, the university and local government. The aim of the centre is to enhance the tourist industry in the region and increase tourism by at least 10% by 2001. It is estimated that this would generate an extra 1 500 direct and indirect tourism jobs (mainly in the hotel and restaurant trade) to complement the existing 17 000 jobs in tourism. The centre is also involved in transferring research into practical knowledge for the numerous small firms which work in the tourism industry in the region. It also plans to establish local field stations which will act as resources to allow the development and diversification of small businesses in the region.

Historically, the South Yorkshire region of England, and its industrial centre Sheffield, has been intimately connected with the metal and steel industries. Building upon these historic strengths, the University of Sheffield has established the Materials Forum as part of the activities of its regional office. The forum is a club for leading edge materials processing companies which work together with the university on over 30 research and development projects. The forum has given rise to several postgraduate projects and interdisciplinary research centres.

HEIs also draw upon their geographical location as a platform for research based activities. In this sense, research activities, expertise and partners can be pooled from wider areas which extend over several national boundaries.

The universities in Eastern Finland draw upon the regional context in a number of research areas. Links with neighbouring Russia were seen as an opportunity for the three universities in Eastern Finland. In particular, the University of Lappeenranta has appointed a professor specialising in Russia and transitional economies and Joensuu has an East-West Innovation Centre and provides training in Russian language for SMEs.

Another important way in which research at HEIs is connected to the regional environment is through donated professorial posts. These are generally in applied fields and reflect the needs and hopes which industry and local society place upon HEIs.

At the University of Newcastle in Northern England, a chair in Micro-Electronics has been established with funding from the Tyne and Wear Development Company. The regional recycling industry and resource management sector in Kassel, Germany, has provided funds for a chair in Resource Management and Recycling Economy at the University of Kassel. Further, Florida Atlantic University in the United States has established eminent scholar chairs through public-private match funding in areas such as community education and nursing.

HEIs are also helping localities to respond to the needs of footloose global investment, by for example, providing training and advice to meet the needs of inward investors. However, the results of responding to these newer regional needs is unclear considering the risks of disinvestment associated with such activity.

The University of Sunderland in the United Kingdom is home to the Sunderland Business School. Within this, the Japanese Studies Division provides Japanese language and business training for a number of clients which reflects new regional demands from the large number of firms from South-East Asia that have invested heavily in the region such as Nissan and Fujitsu.

Research interfaces

- ◆ Does HEI research policy have a regional dimension?
- ◆ Does the technology transfer office have a regional as well as an international and national role?
- ◆ What mechanisms (science parks, incubators, patent offices, etc.) have been developed to commercialise the research base of the HE sector and promote technology transfer between the HEI and regional stakeholders?
- ◆ Is provision made to meet specific skills needs, such as those from SMEs?

A number of recent trends have encouraged HEIs to develop various mechanisms to commercialise their research base and link their research and expertise more closely to the external environment. These trends include:

- The increasing complexity of the technological base of firms which has led them to seek external sources of technology and knowledge to maintain competitiveness.
- The shift of policy attention towards SMEs as vehicles to secure economic success, especially those in high-tech growing sectors.
- Demands from the public sector to see a return on their investment in the research base of HEIs in terms of increased competitiveness of national economies. Similarly, HEIs are keen to offset core funding cuts through increased earnings from research.

The transfer of research between HEIs and other stakeholders is a complex process. Rather than regarding research and knowledge transfer as a simple linear model between HEIs and their partners, there are a number of simultaneous flows between clusters of stakeholders and HEIs which occur on a spectrum from individual and ad-hoc interaction and consultancy work to centrally organised activities. Explicit mechanisms through which research is transferred between HEIs and regional stakeholders include research centres, spin-off companies, incubator units, advice and training services, science parks and mechanisms to exploit intellectual property rights (IPR). However, there needs to be a recognition that the most effective technology and knowledge transfer mechanism between HEIs and the external environment is through the teaching function of HEIs; that is to say through staff and students via the teaching curriculum, placements, teaching company schemes, secondments, etc. This reinforces the intimate relationship between the teaching and research functions of HEIs.

Research interfaces can be considered as a developing "dual structure" within most HEIs in which basic units such as departments are supplemented by new units and forms of activity linked to the outside world. They are responsible for introducing new ideas and promoting a more entrepreneurial culture in HEIs which have spread to more traditional units such as academic departments. These interfaces depend more upon entrepreneurially-sought, locally and regional based funding sources and collaboration with a wide range of partners to capture such funds. Moreover, new research interfaces are challenging existing HEI structures and management forms, especially in terms of introducing entrepreneurialism into traditional disciplinary-bound departments.

Some of the most successful examples of technology transfer and various outreach mechanisms are found within larger and metropolitan universities whose research activities are underpinned by a large state supported research infrastructure. Moreover, there is evidence to show that HEI-industrial contacts are largely non-local in nature and bring together international rather than exclusively regional partners. However, most HEIs have developed explicit and pro-active strategies to support knowledge and research transfer to the regional economy. The following sections illustrate some of the different ways in which research interfaces have been established.

Institutional mechanisms for research transfer

Central institutional mechanisms are a prerequisite for co-ordinating effective technology transfer from HEIs to the region and have the benefit of simplifying access for those wishing to tap into their research base. Many HEIs have established "single-entry points" through which regional stakeholders can access the research base of the institution.

The University of Joensuu in Finland established the "Foundation of the University of Joensuu", a private venture which acts as a stockholder in companies working with knowledge transfer from the university to the region. The foundation was established from donations of regional organisations. It works with firms involved in the science park, which is a legally separate company from the university, and received support from the city and the Association of North Karelian Municipalities. Although the science park is relatively small with 50 firms, it participates in Finland's Innovation Relay Centre Enterprise which exists to transfer technology on a European basis. The regional AMK institution is also involved in the park.

The University of Newcastle in Northern England has developed two successful and regionally appropriate technology transfer mechanisms. The first mechanism, "Knowledge House" (KH), is co-ordinated between all the universities in the North-East and functions as a front door for SMEs which want to access the university's expertise. The second mechanism is the "Regional Centre for Innovation in Engineering Design" (RCID) which, in collaboration with two other regional universities, the University of Northumbria at Newcastle and Sunderland, offers engineering design facilities and services to around 15 of the region's most innovative SMEs. The RCID works on a cluster basis and could be replicated in some of the region's other growth areas such as offshore technology and microelectronics.

The University of Tromsø in Northern Norway is involved in several initiatives to strengthen the interface between the university and regional industry. The university is involved in NORUT, the regional research institute which is one of several national organisations which act as links between universities and regional industry and government. It is also involved in the Tromsø Research Park and several individual technology transfer initiatives such as TEFT which offers SMEs subsidised advice; FORNY which encourages external spin-offs; SMB-kompetanse which encourages SMEs to employ graduates; and REGINN to develop the regional innovation system.

Region-wide co-ordination of initiatives within several HEIs can have the value-added benefits of pooling research funds and expertise which creates economies of scale and avoids duplication.

The Scottish Universities Research Policy Consortium was established from the Scottish Higher Education Funding Council's (SHEFC) Regional Strategic Initiative Fund (RSIF). The objective of the consortium is to enable the thirteen Scottish universities to collaborate on policy for the institutional management of research from which each institution could draw elements relevant to its local needs. An officer and several workshops disseminate information on issues relating to exploiting and managing regionally based research.

Through RSIF, the CONNECT programme was established to foster the exploitation of Scotland's strong research base and to develop technology-based ventures. Based on a model from San Diego, the United States, and initiated by the University of Edinburgh, CONNECT is now supported by several other Scottish universities, the Scottish Higher Education Funding Council, economic development agencies, business advisors and financial institutions.

Several collaborative mechanisms have been developed in the North-East of England to draw the regional universities and industrial partners closer together. The regional government office, GO-NE, with the assistance of the European Regional Development Fund (ERDF), played a key role in developing a Regional Innovation and Technology Strategy (RITS) which aims to integrate the region's universities with the needs of industry. This strategy was developed in collaboration with the North-East Technology Support Network (NETS) which brings together a number of university-based schemes.

Higher Education Support for Industry in the North-East (HESIN) is a consortium of the six universities in the North (along with the Open University) which co-operates closely with the Regional Technology Centre (RTC), local industry and agencies to provide vocational training forum for co-ordination of technology transfer. HESIN has been closely involved with several inward investment decisions in the region. The RTC North is one of a national network of independent technology transfer centres helping to bridge links between academia and industry.

Research centres

HEIs are extremely active in creating research centres as a complement to established discipline-bound departments. Research centres are often multi-disciplinary and draw upon a number of external partners and, as a result, are an effective mechanism to bring HEIs into closer contact with their region.

At the University of New England, Australia's oldest regional university, the university provides a number of services to the rural community through several research centres which include the Agricultural Business Research Institute, the Animal Genetics and Breeding Unit, the Rural Development Centre and the Centre for Water Policy Research.

Sunderland University in the North-East of England has established the Industry Centre which is a wholly owned subsidiary company through which the full range of university services can be managed. This resulted as part of a collaboration between the business leadership team, the Wearside Opportunity and the university. The centre consists of a number of commercial ventures which provide training, consultancy and manufacturing services, research expertise and business services. These include the Advanced Manufacturing Systems Centre, the Decision Support Systems Centre, the Micro Training Centre, the Magnet Centre and the Make IT Grow Initiative aimed at improving the IT capabilities of 100 local companies.

In Australia, the "Co-operative Research Centre Programme" was established by the Commonwealth government in 1990 and now funds 62 collaborative research ventures in the fields of engineering and natural sciences between the universities, the public sector and business. Activities focus upon developing links between university research specialisms and the needs of the regional economy. Such links can be seen at Northern Territory University where research at the centre focuses upon beef and cattle, at the University of Tasmania with research into timber and fishing and at the University of New England with research into wool and cotton production and meat quality.

Warwick University in the United Kingdom represents a well developed university-industry interface and is extremely pro-industry which stemmed from a strong desire in the West Midlands region of England to have a "relevant university". As a result, the university developed strong links with the region's engineering and automobile industries. The university established the Warwick Manufacturing Group (WMG), which was quickly established as Europe's biggest postgraduate centre for engineering R-D. WMG has effectively and profitably linked the activities of the university's engineering department with industry.

Licensing

HEIs can connect research to the external environment by exploiting intellectual property rights. Royalties can be earned from patenting and licensing the processes and products which result from research at HEIs. However, licensing interfaces are likely to be non-local due to the difficulties of matching products/inventions to the capabilities of firms within the regional economy.

The University of Strathclyde in Scotland established a Research and Consultancy Services Office (RCS) which focuses upon the broader notion of "commercialising the research base" of the university rather than the more limited role of technology transfer. The route taken by RCS was based upon exploiting the patenting and licensing of university research rather than fostering spin-outs. As a result, Strathclyde was one of the first universities to seriously exploit the potential within intellectual property. Initially, the university prospered through royalties from patents in pharmaceutical chemistry, but has now diversified its portfolio to over 100 products. £25 million has been earned in the last twelve years from royalties, which equates to £0.15 of royalty for every £1 of research funding expenditure. The university believes that investing in the development of technology and taking up equity in IPR is often better than investing in early stage high-tech start-ups.

Spin-outs and science parks

Increasingly, HEIs are commercialising their research base by encouraging spin-out activities from research. Several different models have been used to capitalise on this "spin-out" phenomenon. Financial support has been granted to encourage entrepreneurship and incubators and science parks have been established to allow such entrepreneurship to flourish.

Science parks have become a well-used and documented phenomenon to promote the growth of entrepreneurialism and SMEs within the regional economic development process. Many are populated with campus companies in which HEIs are a major stakeholder. Science parks can be developed around certain industrial clusters which draw upon the specific competitive advantages of the region's industry and HEI teaching and research profiles. However, it should be acknowledged that science parks are not always the best route for regional development and HEIs must develop interfaces appropriate to the regional context in order for the university-research interface to be managed successfully. Although a vast number of HEIs are now involved in science parks many are often property developments within which the services offered by the HEIs are second to the quality of the built environment. Moreover, it is essential to gauge the net employment impact and whether jobs created are a result of labour displacement from elsewhere in the region.

The University of Adelaide has established the Thebarton Research and Development Centre which is one of Australia's largest university-owned and managed science parks. There are now 30 commercial tenants, eight research groups, eight incubator businesses and over 400 people including 80 postgraduate staff at the centre. The university has generated a return on its investment by utilising derelict land and buildings for the provision of subsidised R-D facilities.

Lappeenranta University in Eastern Finland established the Kareltek Technology Centre in an attempt to diversify the economic base of the region which is heavily dependent upon the forestry industry, to improve the low regional formation rates of SMEs, and to provide more regional employment opportunities for its engineering graduates. There are currently 70 enterprises employing 450 people in the centre, half of which graduated from the university. The centre has made a significant contribution to high-tech spin-off firms around the university, which has been enhanced by the revival of Finnish-Russian trade. Further, such initiatives have created opportunities for engineering graduates to seek employment regionally rather than losing them to the Uusimaa province of Southern Finland.

The Western Australian government established the Western Australian Technology Park in conjunction with the four universities in Western Australia. Activity at the park focuses upon software/innovation technology, mining and pharmaceuticals. The park now employs over 1 000 people and is being used as a model to develop other parks in Australia.

The University of Kuopio in Eastern Finland established a science park which brings together the Neulanen Research Centre, the Regional Public Health Institute, the Finnish Institute of Occupational Health and the Geological Survey of Finland. Taken together, these institutions comprise a specialist expert community of over 1 000 people including postgraduates. The park has helped the university consolidate its reputation as a centre for excellence in health research.

Warwick University in the United Kingdom is involved in Warwick Science Park which houses 65 firms and 1 300 employees on 42 acres. The park has been so successful that a number of satellite parks in the nearby region have been discussed and there is an expanding programme which involves undergraduates in science-based firms. In collaboration with Warwickshire County Council, the Innovation Centre has been created at Warwick Science Park to extend the features of the university and the science park to smaller or start-up technology based, innovative businesses, mainly through offering small, managed workspaces.

An evolving interface

Many HEIs have approached their contribution to regional development through a multi-faceted approach which combines a number of the above mechanisms which in turn reflect the evolving needs of the region. The research relationship between an HEI and its region must therefore be a dynamic one utilising a diversity of tools – spin-outs, science parks, centres of excellence and other gateway mechanisms, and last but not least, teaching and learning through work based experience and professional development which is linked to research. For the relationships to succeed there must be mutual benefits for university researchers and their local partners, whereby research informs practice and practice informs research.

The University of Twente was established in 1961 and charged with the task of developing close links with industry in order to aid the development of the Enschede region in Eastern Netherlands, a marginal and old industrial region facing economic decline. A number of mechanisms were established to promote spin-offs from the university, all of which are co-ordinated through a Liaison Group. Firstly, Temporary Entrepreneurial Placements (TOP) were established to give young entrepreneurs a part-time post in the university to allow them to develop new ventures. TOP is co-financed by EU money and the university is being asked to develop structures like TOP in other European universities. As firms evolved at the university, they then moved out into the university's local government-funded firm incubator, the Business and Technology Centre (BTC), and then finally to Twente Business and Science Park, which is owned by the municipality of Enschede. It is estimated that 300 spin-off firms were assisted and 1 900 new jobs were created from the initiative over the last couple of decades.

The spin-off process at the university is aided by other mechanisms such as Technology Circle Twente (TKT), a group of some hundred young high-tech firms in the region, and the University Spin-off scheme (UNISPIN) to implement workshops and a regional plan for spin-offs.

Chalmers University of Technology in Sweden has created a number of departments, foundations and companies to develop co-operation with industry. Firstly, the Chalmers Industrial Technology Foundation, markets, sells and carries out commercially-applied research and development and specially-designed continuing professional development programmes. Secondly, the Chalmers Innovation Centre Foundation (CIC), provides researchers who wish to start spin-off companies or apply for patents with assistance with management and marketing. CIC also includes an incubator building, a venture capital firm and an Industrial Contact Group to provide companies with information concerning the work of the university.

Further, the Chalmers Science Park Foundation, creates conditions for close co-operation between research departments at major companies and researchers at Chalmers Science Park. The science park is sponsored by the university, local government and the regional chamber of commerce. Finally, the CHAMPS (Chalmers Advanced Management Programmes) Foundation, exists to arrange continuing professional development programmes in technology management for managers in industry. The links between Chalmers University and local industry have also benefited from an initiative from the Swedish National Board for Industrial and Technical Development (NUTEK) which aims to establish competence centres funded jointly by universities, NUTEK and local industry. Chalmers now has six centres which have developed extremely close links with industry.

8

Community Service Management

HEIs and the "third role"

The contributions that HEIs have always made to civil society through the extra-mural activities of individual staff (*e.g.* in the media, politics, the arts, advising government bodies, socio-economic and technological analyses) and through providing liberal adult education and evening classes and access to facilities like libraries, theatres, museums and public lectures are being bundled together and recognised as a "third role" alongside teaching and research. Perhaps more than the other roles, it is this third role of community service which embeds HEIs in the region. In certain contexts, this role reflects the nineteenth century paternalism of industrialists and philanthropists who gave endowments to establish HEIs in their home area in order to create a "cultured" and "civilised" local and regional population. In other contexts, this service role to the local community stems from the obligations on HEIs which arise from being major recipients of local taxes.

However, a number of trends are converging which are increasing this historic service role of HEIs. These can be understood through the interplay of globalisation and localisation as discussed in Chapter 2. Firstly, the increasing awareness of the global, or at least pan-national, nature of problems such as environmental degradation, poverty and economic development has created a number of inter-connected local responses throughout the world to tackle specific issues – thus the rise of the rubric for action, "think globally, act locally" and policy measures such as "Local Agenda 21". Second, is the rise of the local state and local voluntary/community groups in response to the declining influence of, and disillusionment with, national structures. Moreover, fiscal constraints at the level of both local and national government are creating partnerships between the public, private and voluntary sectors in order to govern communities.

The relevance of HEIs to these trends are two-fold. Firstly, HEIs, because of their multi-territoriality and inter-disciplinarity, are institutions which are adequately placed to interpret global issues on a global scale. Secondly, HEIs, their staff and students, are heavily involved in community service through volunteering, project work, mentoring, leadership and commentary. In sum, through this third role of service, HEIs can become one of several actors involved in the governance of local civic society. Clearly, the extent to which these processes

OECD 1999

manifest themselves varies between regions and HEIs. Nevertheless, what the third role highlights is the increasing embeddedness of HEIs in their regions and their duty as responsible local, as well as national and international agents. The following sections highlight some of the ways in which HEIs are undertaking this service role.

The civic and leadership role of HEIs

♦ What role do HEIs play in regional leadership?
♦ Do HEIs participate in local growth coalitions and facilitate inward investment?
♦ What role do HEIs play in providing commentary and critique in the region?
♦ What is the status of HEIs – neutral broker, mediator, active participant, critic?

HEIs can undertake an active role in the community. Regional development and promotional organisations are increasingly looking towards HEIs to provide leadership, analysis, resources and credibility. In this sense, HEIs contribute to the less tangible aspects of the development process by building social networks that link key actors in the local community and feed intelligence into these networks. HEI participation can inject an element of unbiased and informed realism into such networks. Furthermore, the "partnership principle" is increasingly a prerequisite for securing certain forms of funding and for creating an effective platform for enhancing inward investment activity.

HEIs can pursue many different roles in the community. Considering the multiple nature of relationships and institutions with which they can engage, HEIs are not characterised as having a narrow sectional interest by regional stakeholders. Nevertheless, HEIs have to decide what profile to adopt. This could vary from honest broker, impartial/detached observer, active participant or fearless critic.

There are several examples from Australia where HEIs are engaged in regional economic development leadership organisations. For example, the University of Western Sydney provides office infrastructure for the North Western Sydney Regional Economic Development Organisation, the chairperson of which is an executive of the university; Southern Cross University in Northern New South Wales has established the Southern Cross Research Institute as a joint partnership with the Northern Rivers community to undertake research on the regional economy; Deakin University played a key role in the establishment of the Greater Green Triangle Development association in South Australia; and finally, all the universities in South Australia are involved in the Leadership Institute which develops leadership skills in the region.

HEIs provide the region with commentary, analysis, information and access to wider networks, through mechanisms such as media links and public lectures. They also provide analysis of the region's distinctive competitive advantage and help design regional strategies. Staff and students provide key leaders in local civic society by participating in voluntary activities, interpreting world affairs in the regional media and undertaking strategic analysis of the regional economy and society.

> The National University of Ireland, Cork in the South-West of Ireland, established a Regional Strategy Initiative (RSI) in 1992 at about the same time that the Irish government established regional authorities. The RSI operated through a partnership with the new regional authority, county and city governments and the chamber of commerce and the RSI was heavily involved in the regional authority's 5-year action plan. This partnership decided to undertake medium to long range research into problems of sustainable development in peripheral regions. As a consequence, three Masters level fellowships and two PhD fellowships were established from funds provided by each of the partners. The RSI also publishes a *Regional Link* newsletter which disseminates information pertinent to regional development issues in the South-West of Ireland.

> At the University of Newcastle upon Tyne in North-East England, the Centre for Urban and Regional Development Studies (CURDS) has a particular concern for the region, involving itself with issues of structural economic change, labour market intelligence and the influences of new information and communication technologies, but also undertakes work on a European and national basis. CURDS is also the source of many major texts on the North-East and publishes the *Northern Economic Review* jointly with neighbouring universities.

HEIs also provide a framework through which ideas and cultures can be shared and transmitted. In this sense, HEIs can play an important role in opening up and internationalising regions.

> Several HEIs in the Catalan region of Spain are involved in the Barcelona 2004 Forum, a new international event for Catalan society. Under the slogan, "Culture for Peace", the forum will be a meeting point for debate and reflection on culture, peace and sustainable development. HEIs will contribute by working in several scientific and cultural projects in fields such as language and communication, new technologies and urbanism.

HEIs and community service

- ◆ What is the nature and extent of student involvement in voluntary and charity work in the local community?
- ◆ Are there any mechanisms within the HEI through which students can find out about volunteering and community action opportunities in the region?
- ◆ Are there any mechanisms which formally link community service to the academic curriculum?

Another aspect of the third role of HEIs is their role in community and voluntary action in the region. In particular, the student population represents a significant resource to the local community in terms of volunteer workers. In many ways, the United States leads the way in terms of student community service through the "education for citizenship" model. This partly reflects the historic legacy of municipality throughout the federal states and the tradition of Land Grant universities which are dedicated to serving the community. Two official programmes exist to integrate community service within the university curriculum in the United States: Campus Compact and the Campus Outreach Opportunity League (COOL). Community service in the United States is also promoted through AmeriCorps, the Peace Corps (placing students outside the United States) and President Clinton's National Service Scheme under which students earn entitlements to financial aid for their studies by conducting community service.

The University of Wisconsin-Madison in the United States has been able to establish the Morgridge Centre, a front-door interface for the university's community service activities, through a US$ 3.5m contribution from two alumni. The centre will house the Alumni Foundation, along with the Office for Student Volunteers (OSV) and the Dean of Students Office, and is to be located at the centre of the campus to increase the profile of public service to the community from the university. It will have three main roles: to support and enhance the learning environment by creating partnerships that link academic study with community service; serve as a clearinghouse of information about service opportunities at the university; and support student initiatives and leadership by promoting participation in service facilities. The centre reinforces the university's commitment to serving the community as part of its role as a Land Grant institution.

Student community and volunteer action in the United Kingdom is organised by Student Community Action (SCA). There are 125 SCA groups in UK HEIs which provide over 15 000 volunteers from the student body and generate an estimated economic value from their voluntary activity of £9.6 million. SCA groups are a powerful, but often neglected, force within the non-governmental and voluntary sectors in the community. SCA involves students in a range of activities such as working with children, people with disabilities and single parents, contributing to environmental schemes and mentoring in local schools. Moreover, the annual Rag week at British universities contributes around £2 million to SCA projects, all of which goes back into the community. Rag fund-raising helps to cement student-community links.

HEIs and regional resources

♦ What HEI resources/facilities can the regional community access?
♦ What are the financial/time conditions upon such access?
♦ Do HEIs monitor public access to their resources/facilities?
♦ Have HEIs established mechanisms through which their stock of cultural facilities can be jointly managed and marketed to the regional community?

HEIs own a number of facilities such as libraries, sports facilities and arts and cultural venues. These are often significant regional facilities which offer, at a charge, public access and can have a significant impact upon the region in terms of income and employment generation. Since the funding for such facilities at many HEIs is discretionary and not provided for in ear-marked government block-grants, their economic viability often depends upon partnership, especially financial-based ones, with regional stakeholders. Regional access to facilities at HEIs may be a more pressing issue in peripheral areas which have less developed educational, social and cultural infrastructures.

Warwick Arts Centre is part of the University of Warwick in the United Kingdom and is the largest arts centre of its kind in Britain attracting around 250 000 visitors each year and includes a concert hall, two theatres, a cinema, art gallery, music centre and bookshop. The Warwick Arts Centre is responsible for bringing the community into the university on a massive scale and has overcome some of the problems of isolation of this green-field institution from the local community.

In Florida, the United States, the Fort Lauderdale Arts and Sciences District was developed with administrators from Florida Atlantic University (FAU) serving on development boards, advisory boards and political action committees. The US$ 55 million complex consists of a Performing Arts Centre which shows national musicals and pop artists as well as university productions. This district, along with other cultural facilities at FAU, create a significant economic impact upon the surrounding region which was estimated at US$ 140 million.

HEIs offer many resources to the region through their students' unions (SUs). SUs primarily exist to serve the university population, but most offer access to facilities and events to a wider audience through the use of public entertainments licences and conditional liquor licences. In this way, many SUs play a central role in entertainment provision in the region by providing comedy, live-music, dance events and late-night drinking. In particular, SUs can help to increase the cultural reputation of a city or region by functioning as a major entertainment venue.

However, SUs can be caught in the same net of funding cutbacks as HEIs as a whole. In this sense, SUs face the option of expanding their entertainment portfolio to ensure their future financial viability or face closure through successive rounds of cuts to their block grant. In many cases, SUs have embarked upon entrepreneurial activity to strengthen their financial position by raising "third stream" funds and expanding into major entertainment providers, often in partnership with other regional partners, to reach a wide audience throughout the region.

> The University of Coventry in Britain has recently spent £2.5 million to develop a state-of-the-art night-club called The Planet in the city-centre. This development was part of a strategy by the students' union to generate extra revenue and to expand away from the existing inadequate premises on campus. The night-club runs on a membership basis and offers membership to the public. This investment in non-academic activity reflects the ability of Coventry SU to gauge changing consumer demand amongst the city's youth population and to respond to this in order to financially gain from the growing lucrative night-time entertainment market.

HEIs often own and manage facilities of regional interest and value which document aspects of regional culture. In this role, HEIs are cultural custodians of the life of the region. However, there are few funds, especially government ones, to support such activity. In this context, regional and local funding sources can be vital to maintain such facilities. It may be beneficial for HEIs to jointly manage and market their range of arts, cultural and social facilities which are open to the public through an independent consortium comprised of academics, practitioners and venue managers.

> The University of New England, Australia, houses the Historical Resources Centre, a major resource for any historical research carried out on the New England region. It records the activities of the earliest settlers and holds material concerning Aboriginal culture. It also houses the Aboriginal Cultural Centre and Keeping Place, which aims to strengthen and renew Aboriginal culture and improve relationships between the Aboriginal and wider communities.

Regional collaboration and division of labour between HEIs and their facilities can be crucial to maintaining access to vital resources, especially in peripheral or rural areas which have low levels of access to facilities such as libraries and IT services. As in the area of teaching and research it is often necessary for HEIs within a region to work together with external partners in developing a portfolio of facilities and services which can be tailored to regional needs. Regional funding levered in this way can widen the range of facilities available on campus to students, so enhancing the learning experience; at the same time active engagement in the community can enrich the life of both students and teachers. In short, the third role is not a one way street.

> The three universities in Eastern Finland are collaborating to provide access to library resources in this scarcely populated area. The libraries at each of the three universities are very different which reflects the specialist nature of each university and means that inter-university lending is an important function for the libraries. Library services are available free to open university students, AMK institution students, local schools and hospitals and other private members.

9

Conclusions

Drivers/barriers to regional engagement

This report has highlighted the influence of different regional and national settings on the ability to respond to regional needs. In this sense, each HEI has to confront its own set of drivers and barriers to engagement. These will be determined by the characteristics of the national and regional context and the institution's own evolution.

A recent survey of UK universities asked senior managers to identify the most important drivers and barriers to greater regional engagement. The most important drivers were access to new sources of funding, the need to widen access and easier engagement with users of research. However, there was a marked difference between the "old" and "new" university (ex-polytechnic) sectors in that the former prioritised its research function as one of the main drivers, whilst the latter emphasised its teaching role. In terms of barriers, the most important included limited funding streams for regional engagement, lack of commitment/incentive for staff and the large number of regional stakeholders.

The following sections highlight a number of drivers and barriers to the adoption of greater regional engagement which may be common to a number of HEIs in different national and regional contexts.

Drivers for adoption of regional development role

Teaching

- Historical roots linking the institution firmly to its local economic base, its city or local authority which may or may not coincide with a formally defined region.
- To attract inward investment of firms with potential to collaborate with academics.

OECD 1999

- To increase the uptake of graduates into employment within the region in order to enhance key institutional performance indicators, and likelihood of building collaborations with firms.
- To increase postgraduate, professional development and part-time teaching in order to attract more revenue.
- Recruitment of senior management on to boards of regional agencies and initiatives.
- To engage in revenue-earning regional initiatives which demonstrate flexibility in offering new provision.
- More undergraduate students studying from home to avoid debts.
- To create new "ladders of opportunity" for students through access, franchise, compact, and other arrangements.
- More demand from eligible mature and non-traditional students, who are rooted in the region and likely to stay in it.
- Momentum created by significant levels of graduate placement in local firms and students involved in the local economy through part-time jobs, placements, vacation work and project work.

Research

- Perceived thrust of government policy towards promoting industrial links.
- Regionalisation of national technology development and transfer policy in regional fora concerned with economic development.
- Demand from government and others for HEI involvement as a precondition of competitively awarded industrial assistance.
- The close links between HEIs and the health sector.
- In the context of Europe, ERDF/ESF funding.

Barriers to adoption of a regional development role

Teaching

- Demand for courses which are not particularly congruent with the development needs of the region – at least as defined by existing agencies.
- Government caps on the number of publicly funded students which can lock HEIs into an historic pattern of nationally-driven subject provision.
- Weakly developed regional economic development strategies which embrace all actors.
- Academic promotion and other reward systems which work against investment of time in design and delivery of professional development short courses, non-award bearing initiatives, or more open/distance learning opportunities.
- Content and mode of delivery of courses at undergraduate (UG) and postgraduate (PG) level determined by external accreditation from professional bodies with little regard for regional development needs.

- Anxiety about the "decline in standards" believed to be attendant on the increased diversity of course provision at undergraduate (UG) and postgraduate (PG) levels and a consequent desire for stiffer national/international benchmarking.
- Too few executive/implementation links between the senior management team and individual academics such that regional policy initiatives agreed by senior management team members are not in fact followed through at the level of teaching.
- Formula for funding teaching not reflecting any regional criteria.
- Costs of regional collaborative projects which have high start-up costs or require substantial amounts of time from senior staff and offer only short term funding.
- Perception that new programmes which address regional needs at undergraduate level can only be introduced at the expense of established programmes.
- Insufficient regional funding to bear the full costs of developing new programmes.
- Too few stakeholders willing to contribute to the development of a pool of high level skills in the region, fearing that enhanced skills only make people more mobile and therefore part of national and international, rather than regional, labour markets.
- Shortage of publicly funded postgraduate studentships with the distribution of those which exist historically determined with little or no account taken of regional needs in their allocation.
- Difficulty of matching the attributes of graduates and the skill needs of local employers, especially SMEs.

Research

- Research agenda heavily influenced by the research councils and national government priorities.
- Academic staff promotion depending on original research of national/international significance with no incentive for applying the research findings to the solution of problems in local companies.
- The absence of linkages between policy formation at senior management team level and the research agendas adopted by individuals and groups lower in the hierarchy (who have a less well developed sense of corporate identity) which weakens the effectiveness of "agreed" regional priorities.
- Base funding for research in HEIs is selective, and likely to get more so, to the advantage of institutions in the "superleague" who tend not to have regional concerns at the heart of their mission.
- Research funding from the EU R-D framework programmes, from national government departments and from most charities does not generally require or reward a close identification with regional development or regional issues.

- Research sponsors base their funding decisions mainly on the quality and on the reputation of key individuals; regional impact is not taken into account. They do not necessarily fund such research in HEIs in areas which have particular developmental needs.
- Regional agencies do not command sufficient funds to commission research programmes of substance focused on regional needs.
- Judgement of research quality by academic peers is deeply entrenched. This may militate against the success of projects that have a regional focus either because they look parochial, or because they are replicative of work elsewhere rather than breaking new ground, or because they look too "applied" as opposed to "basic".
- The informal networks which usually can be powerful determinants of the success or otherwise of research have a national, and international, base maintained through research conferences or subject associations, the external examiner system, and co-membership of national committees.
- Funding from industry tends to come from R-D units at headquarters rather than reflecting the needs of branch units. This is a particular problem in peripheral regions where there are very few R-D units belonging to big companies.

Emerging institutional forms

What is evident from this discussion of the response of HEIs to regional needs is the emergence of new management and institutional forms. It is evident that some HEIs are changing in response to a number of external threats, in particular as they lose their monopolistic position as teaching, research and community service providers. Thus a much wider range of players are now involved in the provision of functions which were traditionally the preserve of the university. In terms of teaching, the lifelong learning agenda suggests that learning occurs everywhere and is not limited to the classroom; in terms of research, a host of public and private institutes, think tanks and policy units disseminate information and expertise; and in terms of service, a plethora of organisations from the public, private and voluntary sectors are involved in community activity.

Many HEIs are responding to these threats through a process of institutional evolution. A variety of terms have been used to describe this transformation such as "entrepreneurial", "responsive", or "learning organisation". However, the extent to which HEIs are adopting new institutional forms varies widely. At one end of the spectrum are the older, more traditional universities which have been detached from their localities and at the other are the more self-consciously local and regional, and often newer, institutions who are at the forefront of institutional evolution. HEIs which embrace characteristics from both sides of this divide face greater problems of institutional re-engineering in order to retain a balanced portfolio of activities. But for institutions of all types there can be little doubt that one of the key drivers for institutional charge is the demand for greater regional engagement.

The concept of the "learning region" has been central to this report. Within the learning region, HEIs have a clear role to play and an incentive to participate, not least because the regional agenda provides a focus for the creation of more responsive, entrepreneurial and learning institutions of higher education that are seen to be meeting societal demands. So, there is a fortunate concordance between the interests of universities and the interests of regions. This concordance has been neatly captured by Duke in his keynote address to an IMHE conference on lifelong learning – a statement which provides a fitting conclusion to this report:

"For universities, the learning region may be the best kept secret of the dying days of this century. In practical terms this implies blending and combining competition in the "new enterprise environment" with collaboration; fostering and supporting "boundary spanners" who can work across the borders of the university in effective discourse with other organisations and their different cultures; fostering cultural change to enable universities to speak and work with partners from many traditions and persuasions as more learning organisations emerge and together enrich their various overlapping learning zones or regions. "

10

Recommendations

To national governments

In unitary states without regional structures of governance, territorial development poses a fundamental challenge to the division of responsibility between ministries organised on a functional basis. In such situations, enhancing the responsiveness of HEIs to regional needs inevitably requires inter-ministerial dialogue and collaboration. While the primary responsibility for funding universities is likely to rest with the Ministry of Education or a quasi-independent funding body reporting to it, the regional agenda for universities is also likely to touch on the concerns of a number of different ministries – such as industry, science and technology, employment and the labour market, home affairs/local government, and culture and sport. Insofar as these ministries already deal with universities it may be with different parts of the institution (*e.g.* one vice-rector responsible for research and industrial liaison and another for cultural affairs). Thus, HEIs reproduce the functional divisions within the national government. The following discussion focuses on the Education Ministry but with reference to other ministries where appropriate.

The geography of higher education

Just as individual institutions need to undertake their own mapping of regional engagement, so too the Ministry of Education needs to compile basic information on the geography of higher education within the national territory. Whilst most ministries do collect a great deal of statistical information about the characteristics of their higher education system, this often lacks geographical detail. A fundamental task therefore is to identify, for the higher education system as a whole, which courses are taught where, the home origins of students and where graduates enter into the labour market. Such analyses need to be benchmarked against regional data on participation in higher education and industrial and occupational structure to identify areas of under and over provision.

A particular concern of this mapping task will be to identify the steps between different levels of the education system – schools, further/vocational education/community colleges, higher education, postgraduate institutions – in order to assess how far the regional pattern of provision assists/inhibits access and progress of students. In short, geographical analysis should highlight the fact that lifelong learning is an agenda that should be responsive to the needs of *people in places*.

Inter-ministerial dialogue

There is a growing recognition in Ministries of Employment of the link between skills and regional competitiveness. For example in a recent OECD report on this subject the Deputy Secretary General noted that "the economic well-being of nations is embodied in the sum of the economic vitality and competitiveness of regions ... but ... some regions are dynamic and others have to cope with mismatches between industries and institutions". However, whilst there is a developing dialogue between Ministries of Employment and Industry around this agenda, higher education is often absent from the debate. This gap needs to be filled.

In sharp contrast the role of universities in technology transfer, including regional technology transfer, is now well established within Ministries of Technology. In part this has followed from the Silicon Valley phenomenon which has prompted numerous copycat experiments with science parks in universities and in part from a regional policy concern about the uneven distribution of technological development capacity, particularly within the European Union. The fact that technology can be transferred through processes of teaching and learning – and with more certain localised effects – needs to be addressed by a dialogue between Technology and Education Ministries.

A final national agenda in which universities are directly and indirectly involved at a regional level, but in which their contribution is seldom recognised by the relevant ministry, relates to culture and sport. University libraries, museums, art galleries and sport facilities and student audiences and participation in these activities with the university is a major contribution that needs to be recognised, planned for and financially supported.

Incentives and funding programmes for regional development and HEIs

Incentives and funding programmes need to be established to encourage HEIs to establish programmes/projects which have an explicit regional dimension and aim to strengthen co-operative activity within the region. Part of this includes fostering regional forums which bring together a wide range of regional stakeholders.

Moreover, governments need to promote partnerships and dialogue between regional education providers such as schools, FE and HE and other training providers. Such mechanisms are essential to support and encourage a regional learning system, in which educational providers co-operate to contribute to regional development.

To local and regional authorities

Understanding higher education

For many public authorities operating at the local and regional scale, the university remains a "black box". What drives academics as teachers and researchers, the way in which the institution is governed and managed, the mechanisms of central government funding are seldom well understood. Just as it is a key task for HEIs to explain this, so too regional authorities must attempt to learn about higher education. General understanding needs to be supported by detailed knowledge of the research and teaching portfolio of HEIs, such that when opportunities arise – for example, a potential new inward investor – the development agencies can quickly identify the appropriate part of the university to be engaged in the negotiation process. Such mutual knowledge and understanding is a necessary, if not sufficient, condition for effective action which mobilises university resources for regional development.

HEI expertise in regional analysis

Joint research between HEIs and local and regional authorities on the strength and weaknesses of the economy can be a useful way of building the relationship. HEIs are a repository of knowledge about future technological, economic and social trends that need to be harnessed to help the region understand itself, its position in the world and identify possible future directions. HEIs can also act as a gateway to global information and tailor this information to meet the needs of different sectors of the regional economy.

Public authorities need to explore mechanisms with HEIs for tapping into this knowledge base at both strategic and operational levels. In terms of strategy, events like a regional future search conference involving staff drawn from across the university and the public and private sector within the region is one possibility. Such an event might be followed by inviting university staff onto a joint regional strategy formulation team. At an operational level, gateway offices which maintain an expertise data base will need to be established if SMEs and small public and private organisations are to gain access to university knowledge. Last, but not least, public bodies will need to actively recruit university staff onto advisory boards guiding the various aspects of economic and cultural development within the region.

HEI incorporation into regional action plans and programmes

Regional analysis and knowledge transfer must be followed by action plans and programmes which incorporate the expertise of the university. In each of the main themes within a development programme there is likely to be a requirement for active university participation. In the search for inward investment there will be room for university participation in overseas delegations. In regional technological development programmes, there will be opportunities for universities to provide expertise to assist with product and process innovation through consultancies, student placements and management development. In skills enhancement linked to raising regional competitiveness there should be a place for targeted graduate retention and continuing professional development initiatives. In cultural development, there will be scope for joint planning of provision of non-vocational education and of opening up of university facilities to the general public. Finally, in terms of regional capacity building, university staff and facilities can be mobilised to promote public debate.

Financial support for collaborative projects

Just as there is a need for national funding bodies to earmark specific funds to enable HEIs to pursue a third role, regional authorities will likewise need to underpin their requirements for new relationships with HEIs by financial support. This could take many forms but perhaps the most vital need is help for HEIs to establish mechanisms for regional interface that can be sustained on a long-term basis. Many of the initiatives outlined above are resource intensive and place considerable burdens on hard pressed senior management in universities. As more and more sources of funding from national governments and bodies like the European Union relevant to the third role of universities are short term and project based, local or regional authorities could play a key role in ensuring the sustainability of university engagement by financially underpinning the bidding process.

To HEIs

Throughout the OECD the autonomous teaching and research activities of publicly funded universities is coming under increasing pressure from governments and their electorates. The agenda has moved on from a desire to simply increase the general education level of the population and the overall volume of scientific research; there is now a desire to harness university education and research to meet specific economic and social objectives. Nowhere is this demand for specificity more clear than in the field of regional development. While universities are located *in* regions, they are also being required to make a contribution to the development *of* those regions. The concern is therefore not only to identify the passive impact of HEIs in terms of direct and indirect employment but also to create mechanisms through which the resources of universities can be mobilised to contribute to the development process. This undoubtedly amounts to a third role for universities (after teaching and research), the pursuit of which can challenge established traditions of institutional governance. The following paragraphs sketch out a possible programme of action for HEIs wishing to take this role seriously.

Mapping of regional links

The starting point for any response should be a straightforward mapping of regional links in terms of teaching, research and participation in regional public affairs. A very basic task is to identify the home origin of students, what academic programmes they participate in and the destination of graduates by occupation, industry and geographical location. With the judicious use of external data, the university should be able to establish its share of national and regional student and graduate markets, its contribution to raising levels of participation in higher education in the region and graduate skills in the regional labour market. The university should aim to establish mechanisms that track students on a longitudinal basis, including their careers as alumni and use this information to guide the shaping of academic programmes.

On the research side, the geography of collaboration with the users and beneficiaries of research needs to be established. Again, external benchmarks will be required to make sense of these data, for example to identify regional companies and organisations absent from the list. The mapping should identify the participating departments within the university, again to reveal possible missing links.

Finally, the contribution of the university to regional public affairs can be mapped by identifying university staff participating in politics, the media, the voluntary sector, the arts and other educational institutions. An important distinction will need to be made between informal engagement where staff act in an individual capacity and formal university participation in partnership arrangements.

Documenting the present linkages and publicising them within the region will be an important first step in raising the profile of the university. Publicity within the institution will be equally important to draw the attention of all of the staff to the extent and significance of regional engagement. Such documentation is an essential prelude to a self-evaluation of the institution's desire and capacity to respond to regional needs.

Self-evaluation of institutional capacity to respond to regional needs

There are a number of possible dimensions to a self-evaluation:

- *Synthesis*: Does university recognise that by its very nature the territorial development process is broadly based embracing economic, technology, environmental, social, cultural and political agendas? University is capable of contribution to this process across a broad front, not least by highlighting the interconnections across these various areas. Indeed regional engagement provides an opportunity for reasserting the unity of the university as a place-based institution.
- *Focus*: What is the distinctive contribution of the university to the regional agenda? Notwithstanding the potential breadth of its contribution the university will need to prioritise those areas where it can make the most cost-effective contribution to the development of the region.
- *Geographical identity*: What are the unique features of the region to which the university can contribute? While there are global, economic, technological, social and cultural drivers of the development processes, these interact very differently with specific regional development trajectories. The university will need to develop a collectively understanding of its region in order to identify particular opportunities for engagement.

- *Regional policy*: What are the main drivers of regional policy? Regional and national agencies have a suite of policies to address regional development. The university needs to understand these policies and identify areas where it can support and reinforce these policy objectives.
- *Teaching and learning*: Has regional labour market intelligence influenced the shape of teaching and learning programmes? Whilst mechanisms are being put in place in some universities to respond to the regional research agenda, less progress appears to have been made on linking teaching and learning to regional needs.
- *Mainstream*: Has regional engagement become part of the academic mainstream of the university? Whilst many universities have established gatekeeper functions (*e.g.* Regional Development Offices) it remains unclear how far this has influenced mainstream teaching and research.
- *Communications*: Are regional needs and priorities communicated through the university? In addition to strategic engagement, there will be opportunities for regional engagement generated externally and internally that will need to be communicated around the institution. Newsletters, electronic mail and established fora provide an opportunity for such communication.
- *Research and intelligence*: Is the university providing the region with intelligence for its forward planning? In order to shape the regional development agenda the university will need to draw upon its global network and external information and tailor this to regional needs.
- *Responsiveness*: Is the university able to respond quickly to unanticipated regional needs? Economic development is opportunistic as well as strategic. If windows of opportunity (*e.g.* release of a new technology, mobile investment projects, new fiscal incentives, new regulatory regimes) are not seized regionally the advantages will be taken up elsewhere. The university will have to put mechanisms in place to respond, for example with new courses and research programmes.
- *Leadership*: What role does the university play in regional leadership? In addition to responding to established policy, universities have the capacity to set regional and national agendas. This involves more than injecting good ideas into the policy process; it also requires building the institutional capacity to take these ideas forward.
- *Collaboration*: Are procedures in place to support inter-university collaboration? All universities in a region have an interest in raising participation in the lifelong learning process. "Growing the market" is to be preferred to mercantilism and this will involve collaboration within and between levels in the education system, including schools and colleges.
- *Partnerships*: Are the objectives of partnerships clear? Partnerships are for the long-term and need to move beyond the identification of additional sources of funding to dialogue that affects the behaviour of participants.

- *Institutional cultures*: Are the institutional cultures and working practices of HEIs and other regional partners similar enough to allow active engagement and dialogue? Moreover, transdisciplinary units are an important route through which working practices which encourage greater regional engagement can be embedded in the institutional culture.

Answers to these questions are likely to point to changes in organisational structure and processes and these are discussed below.

Establishing internal mechanisms for regional engagement

HEIs are characteristically loosely coupled organisations. Individual academics pursue their own research and teaching agendas, which may or may not involve regional engagement. Senior staff (rectors, vice-rectors, heads of administration) often have a responsibility to represent the university to regional interests but have limited capacity to "deliver" the university or particular parts in relation to evolving external agendas. Various central administrative functions (estates, communications and public affairs, industrial liaison, centres for continuing education, careers guidance services) often engage in quasi autonomous work with regional actors and agencies. Individual vice-rectors/pro vice-chancellors may also deal separately with teaching and with research/industrial liaison.

In these circumstances there is an obvious requirement for the university to establish a regional office close to the rector/president/vice-chancellor. Such an office should:

- Co-ordinate and manage regional links.
- Contribute to marketing of the university.
- Provide an input to strategic planning.
- Contribute to regional marketing.
- Develop frameworks for engagement and regional understanding within the university.
- Maintain pressure for mainstreaming of regional engagement through the normal channels of the institution.

The effectiveness of the activity of the regional office is likely to be fundamentally influenced by the institutional incentives and the award mechanisms to individual academics and departments. These are discussed below.

Review incentives and reward systems

It is widely recognised that the principal allegiance of most academics is to their discipline and not to their institution, with standing amongst peers being largely determined through publications. This standing is reflected within the institution through grading and salary rewards. More recently, some institutions have begun to reward achievement in teaching, drawing upon quality assessments and peer reviews. Universities wishing to encourage staff who are engaged in the regional agenda may therefore wish to consider how some of the indicators used in mapping regional links might be reflected in their internal reward system.

Incentive systems to reward and stimulate staff involvement in activities which assist or co-operate with regional stakeholders need to be established, as well as an ability for national assessments of higher education systems and staff promotional routes to include activities related to regional engagement.

Staff development

One of the key factors of success in regional partnerships is the presence of "animateurs" who act as gatekeepers between different networks and organisations. If universities are to successfully mainstream regional engagement through the institution they will require a number of staff who develop skills as "animateurs". For the most part the necessary skills and attributes are intuitive and learnt through practice; however, some training and support will be required from the university staff development programme. Relevant competencies include: management of change; building and managing networks; facilitation and mediation; working with different organisational cultures; project planning and implementation; raising financial support; self-directed learning; supervision and personal support techniques; organisational politics and dynamics.

Alongside the "know-how" aspects of such a programme, HEIs will need to ensure that the key staff have knowledge of the facts of regional development. These facts include the structure of the organisations involved in regional development; central and local government powers and responsibilities; the different time scales and drivers influencing these organisations; the overlaps between organisations and how these can be used to mutual advantage.

Once they have the skills, the key staff need to mobilise the institution as a whole in an internal dialogue about its future regional role. This dialogue will need to draw upon data collected in the mapping exercise such that the institution learns from a collective analysis of its own position and uses this to inform future behaviour.

Appendix 1
List of HEIs from which material was drawn

Deakin University, Australia
La Trobe University, Australia
Northern Territory University, Australia
Royal Melbourne Institute of Technology, Australia
Southern Cross University, Australia
University of Adelaide, Australia
University of Hawkesbury, Australia
University of New England, Australia
University of South Australia, Australia
University of Western Australia, Australia
University of Western Sydney, Australia

University of Hong Kong, China

Aalborg University, Denmark

Lappeenranta University of Technology, Finland
University of Joensuu, Finland
University of Kuopio, Finland
University of Turku, Finland
University of Vaasa, Finland

National University of Ireland, Cork, Ireland
Tralee Regional Technical College, Ireland

Klaipeda University, Lithuania

University of Twente, Netherlands

Massey University, New Zealand

OECD 1999

University of Tromsø, Norway

Technical University of Catalonia, Spain

Chalmers University of Technology, Sweden
Umeå University, Sweden
University of Mid-Sweden, Sweden

Coventry University, the United Kingdom
Open University, the United Kingdom
University of Bristol, the United Kingdom
University of Edinburgh, the United Kingdom
University of the Highlands and Islands, the United Kingdom
University of Leeds, the United Kingdom
University of Newcastle upon Tyne, the United Kingdom
University of Sheffield, the United Kingdom
University of Strathclyde, the United Kingdom
University of Sunderland, the United Kingdom
University of Warwick, the United Kingdom

Florida Atlantic University, the United States
Florida International University, the United States
University of Miami, the United States
University of Wisconsin-Madison, the United States
Western Governors University, the United States

Appendix 2
Reviews of selected national systems
of higher education

Australia

The Australian higher education sector is predominantly publicly funded, and consists of:

- 36 universities, generally larger institutions which receive operating funds from the Commonwealth under the Higher Education Funding Act (1988) on a triennial basis, and which between them had a total of 667 679 students in 1998.
- 4 other smaller higher education institutions (the Australian Maritime College, Avondale College, Batchelor College and Marcus Oldham College) which receive operating grant funds from the Commonwealth government, and which had a total of 2 235 students in 1998.
- 3 other vocationally specialised smaller institutions [the Australian Film, Television and Radio School (AFTRS), the National Institute of Dramatic Art (NIDA) and the Australian Defence Force Academy (ADFA)] with a total of 1 939 students in 1998, which receive their main operating funds from the Commonwealth government but from portfolios other than the Department of Education, Training and Youth Affairs (DETYA, which funds the universities).
- 2 private universities which do not receive any operating grant funds from the Commonwealth government (Bond University and Notre Dame University), and about 36 other smaller private providers, including theological colleges and providers with specialist interests in particular artistic or vocational fields.

In 1998 therefore the Australian higher education system (excluding the private providers) enrolled 671 853 students (a 2% increase from 1997), of whom 266 712 were commencing students (0.2% increase from 1997). In 1997, 155 137 students completed their award courses in higher education, a 6.7% increase on the previous year, and the publicly funded higher education institutions in Australia employed 70 681 equivalent full-time staff. In 1996, the participation rate in publicly funded Australian higher education was 54‰ of the 17-64 year old population.

In terms of the distribution of students between different states in 1998 amongst the publicly funded institutions, 210 618 students (or 31.3% of all students) were enrolled in 13 higher education institutions in New South Wales; 182 154 students (27.1%) were in 9 institutions in Victoria; 117 919 students (17.6%) were in 6 institutions in Queensland; 65 657 students (9.8%) were in 4 institutions in Western Australia; 48 041 students (7.2%) were in 3 institutions in South Australia; 12 628 students (1.9%) were in 2 institutions in Tasmania; 4 689 students (0.7%) were in 2 institutions in the Northern Territory; 19 941 students (3.0%) were in 3 institutions in the Australian Capital Territory; and the Australian Catholic University, which has a number of campuses in different states across Australia, totalled 10 206 students.

Co-ordination of Commonwealth and state roles in higher education

Most higher education institutions in Australia and universities in particular (except the Australian National University and the Australian Maritime College) are established under state legislation through individual Acts of State Parliaments. So although the Commonwealth government technically does not have constitutional power over higher education it does however have a leading role in higher education policy and administration flowing from its key responsibility for funding public higher education institutions.

A major review of Australian federalism in recent years with agreement through the Council of Australian Governments has described the public higher education system as an area of shared responsibility. The agreement stated that the Commonwealth was to have primary funding and policy-making responsibility, and each state's role was to relate to legislation and governance and to identify broad priorities for the development of the sector, taking account of state-level obligations with respect to other levels of education, regional development, planning and infrastructure provision. Since 1988, Commonwealth-State Joint Planning Committees have operated to provide advice to state and Commonwealth Ministers on matters such as state-specific higher education needs, the source and distribution of higher education resources among the publicly funded institutions within states, other matters such as mergers and rationalisation of institutions and campuses, and cooperation with the Technical and Further Education (TAFE) sector.

Universities therefore deal with both Commonwealth and state governments on a regular basis regarding various levels of government's respective areas of responsibility. National advisory arrangements provide channels through which state governments and other stakeholders influence Commonwealth government decision making on higher education matters. State-Commonwealth consultation occurs at ministerial level through the Ministerial Council on Employment, Education and Training (MCEETYA) and at official level through the Commonwealth-State Joint Planning Committees, while the Australian Research Council (ARC) and the Higher Education Council (HEC) provide formal channels for stakeholder input. The ARC, for example, advised by a number of disciplinary based sub-committees, makes detailed recommendations to the Commonwealth Minister on the allocation of targeted research funds.

In terms of governance and management, Australian universities are autonomous, self-accrediting institutions, established by state legislation (except the two cases above). These legislative acts typically vest responsibility for governance and management in a governing body, in the form of a council or senate, which is accountable to the state government (or in the case of the two institutions above, the Commonwealth) for the operations of the institution. Governing bodies usually have 18-25 members (sometimes up to 40), composed of differing mixes of the Chancellor who is the Chair of the governing board; government ministerial appointees; some parliamentarians; staff and student representatives; other appointees of the Minister; some senior academics (usually the vice-chancellor and the Chair of academic board). The acts also provide for the establishment of the vice-chancellor as the chief executive officer, and for appropriate delegations of authority.

Funding

The main features of Commonwealth funding for higher education comprise:

- Operating resources in the form of a single block operating grant to the institution. A block grant is not split into components for salaries or equipment purchases for example, and is derived from three components: 1) a teaching related component which is the largest part of the operating grant and is determined on the basis of the annual total load target plus the undergraduate load target measured in EFTSU (equivalent full-time student units); 2) the research quantum component, which is allocated on the basis of a composite competitive index which contains assessed elements relating to success in attracting research grants and research performance; 3) a capital component which is a fixed amount.
- Allocation of resources in the context of a rolling triennium. This means that the funding announcements are usually three years in advance, which provides institutions with reasonable funding predictability.
- Additional allocation of research funds for specific purposes, primarily on a competitive basis through several research schemes, most of which are referred to the Australian Research Council for advice on allocations to universities and individual researchers in the forms of large grants, research centres, fellowships, scholarships and infrastructure.
- An accountability framework provided essentially by the yearly submission of "educational profiles"'. An annual round of educational profile discussions is held with individual institutions to address issues such as performance against strategic targets, plans for the triennium and future resource bids. Further elements of the accountability and

reporting framework include financial and statistical reporting by institutions. Summary data from the student, staff and finance collections are published annually in *Selected Higher Education Statistics*. The government has also integrated quality improvement processes into the annual profile negotiations through analyses of individual institutional quality improvement plans.

In 1990, the government released a policy framework for equity in higher education, the main aim of which was to ensure that people from all social groups have the opportunity to participate successfully in higher education by changing the balance of the student population to reflect more closely the composition of society as a whole. Six equity groups were identified and strategic goals were established for each. The groups were: people with a disability; people from socio-economically disadvantaged backgrounds; women, particularly in non-traditional areas of study and in postgraduate courses; people from non-English-speaking backgrounds; Aboriginal and Torres Strait Islander people; and people from rural and isolated areas. Merit based equity scholarships are provided to encourage participation by persons from an educationally disadvantaged background. Responsibility for pursuing equity targets is vested in the universities. Institutions are required to include an equity plan and report on progress in their educational profiles, and receive additional targeted funds based on performance against a number of equity indicators.

In 1998, the Commonwealth provided a total of A$ 5.5 billion in funding to higher education institutions. This comprised A$ 4.9 billion in operating grants, including a capital component of A$ 260 million and a research quantum component of A$ 219 million; A$ 38.2 million for capital projects from the Capital Development Pool; and a competitive research programme totalling A$ 450 million. Estimated total income for Commonwealth-funded institutions in 1998 is A$ 8.05 billion, including revenue from fees and other private activities.

The majority of Australian undergraduate students make a contribution towards the cost of their education through the Higher Education Contribution Scheme (HECS), based on the principle that students should be required to contribute towards the cost of higher education when they have the financial means to do so. From 1998, universities are able to offer fee-paying undergraduate places to Australian students once they have filled their funded Commonwealth targets, but not all institutions have chosen to do so, and initial uptakes in others have been modest (about 800 enrolments in 1998).

At the postgraduate, level full fees may be charged for award courses. Most students in fee paying courses are enrolled in coursework masters degrees or in graduate diploma or certificate courses. The majority of postgraduate scholarship recipients are enrolled in doctorate or masters degrees by research. Overseas students at Australian public universities are charged fees for courses at both the undergraduate and postgraduate level. The Commonwealth sets a minimum fee for overseas students at the level of the full average cost of delivery. This is to ensure that the operating grant from the Commonwealth is not being used to subsidise overseas students.

The Commonwealth government commissioned a major Review of Higher Education Financing and Policy in January 1997 to recommend reforms to equip Australia's higher education sector for the next twenty years, and the Review Committee chaired by Roderick West, released its final report *Learning for Life* in April 1998. The Commonwealth government has indicated its intention to take some time to consider the detailed proposals of the West Committee before making a comprehensive response.

Regional matters

Appendix 12 of the West Committee's 1997 Policy Discussion Paper specifically addressed the economic contribution of regional universities in Australia. A more recent report commissioned by the Commonwealth's Evaluations and Investigations Programme entitled *Creative Associations in Special Places* carried out by Steve Garlick from the Regional Research Institute at Southern Cross University provides a complementary and contrasting source of analyses about the relationship of universities with their regions.

The West Review's final report characterised regional universities in the following way:

"If we think of regional Australia as those areas of Australia which are not centred on a capital city, then Australia's 38 universities include 12 regional universities, 11 public universities and one private university (Bond), of which all but two are based in the two most decentralised States of New South Wales and Queensland. However, the approach taken to the provision of regional university education in Western Australia, South Australia, Tasmania, and for the most part Victoria is in sharp contrast to that in New South Wales and Queensland. Their distinctive approach has been to anchor regional provision in comprehensive regional campuses of capital city based universities." (p. 142)

In contrast to defining "the regional university" as one with a non-metropolitan presence, Garlick uses the concept of "regional" very differently:

"This project has found that some universities in metropolitan regions appear to have a greater economic connectedness with their local and regional economy than do some universities in rural areas." (p. 4)

Given the overall population distribution of Australia, it is not surprising that most HEIs are located in urban areas. The six major cities (Sydney, Melbourne, Brisbane, Adelaide, Perth and Canberra) account for about 54% of the total Australian population, yet HEIs in those six cities accounted for 76% of total student enrolments in 1998. In contrast the twelve regional universities cited in West together accounted for 20.2% of total 1998 enrolments. The eight largest institutions (using EFTSU measures) accounting for nearly 40% of all Australian enrolments in 1998 are based in three cities (Sydney, Melbourne and Brisbane): Monash University (31 260); the University of Sydney (27 750); the University of Melbourne (27 600); Queensland University of Technology (23 800); the University of New South Wales (23 600); the University of Queensland (23 500); the Royal Melbourne Institute of Technology (21 600); the University of Western Sydney (21 470).

West's "regional" institutions are comparatively small and relatively young, with only the University of New England and the University of Newcastle pre-dating the 1960s. West however cited the Australian vice of "urbanism" ("If it's good it must be based in a capital city") and pointed out that the research records of some regional universities were at least comparable with those of capital city universities of similar size and age. The West Review was, in general, supportive of the regional universities and stated that:

> "By and large they have survived and even flourished through their adaptability, their willingness to make intelligent use of the new learning technologies, and strong bonding with their host communities – reflected in a continuing commitment to enrich the cultural and social as well as the industrial and economic well-being of their communities." (p. 143)

However, the West Review highlighted a number of challenges faced by the regional universities. Firstly, they are vulnerable in terms of their relative dependence on the provision of distance education: of Australia's 87 000 equivalent full-time students studying externally in 1997, some 57 000, or 66%, were enrolled at the twelve regional universities. A major challenge for these universities, then, is to achieve economies of scale and enter into high volume markets in order to be able to compete with other providers of flexible and distance education. They may find it difficult to provide competitively priced distance education and flexible learning in the face of growing competition from the larger metropolitan universities offering on-line courses and increasingly from private and international providers.

Secondly, at the same time such universities must do more to increase their numbers of on-campus students within existing infrastructure limitations. Regional universities have been successful in recruiting international fee paying students, and regional universities are well placed to recruit students from their local areas who will benefit from not having to meet the added living costs that they would incur if they attended metropolitan institutions. As the cost of higher education to the individual rises, then study at the local institution is likely to become a more frequent option.

The West Review makes an explicit claim about the responsibility which regional stakeholders have in securing the financial viability of such institutions:

> "Should the financial viability of a regional institution be threatened, it might be possible to mount a "public good" argument for special purpose support, such as additional research infrastructure, on the grounds of the institution's broader significance within the local community. However, this is a regional development issue, not a higher education issue per se. Consideration of any support would need to have regard to other support provided to the region and to prevailing regional development policies. It may be that universities seeking support on the grounds of their non-educational significance to their regions should do so via regional development funding." (p. 145)

The further education sector also plays a well developed role in meeting regional needs in Australia, with the Technical and Further Education institutions (TAFEs) undertaking a strong and well established local economic development role. There are real differences in terms of purpose and operation between the two sectors. Firstly, estimates indicate that public funding per full-time equivalent student for TAFE is, on average, greater in absolute terms than that provided for higher education. Secondly, the existence of separate regulatory and funding arrangements for the two sectors means that the best co-ordinated use may not be made of all the resources available for postsecondary education in Australia. Artificial administrative boundaries may distort students' choices between TAFE and higher education and also affect the way institutions in both sectors respond to student and employer needs. Further, unlike TAFE students, most higher education students in undergraduate courses may defer payment of tuition charges.

However, as students increasingly blur the sectoral boundaries by actively individualising learning pathways, linkages between the vocational education and training sector and the higher education sector have improved significantly during the 1990s with inter-institutional collaboration and co-operative arrangements producing improvements in credit transfer and the recognition of prior learning, the development of co-located and new shared campus arrangements such as at Coffs Harbour and Ourimbah in New South Wales, and cross-sectoral mergers and growth of multi-sectoral institutions in Victoria. Some institutions such as the Royal Melbourne Institute of Technology and the Northern Territory University have operated for many years with a TAFE division successfully incorporated within a recognised university.

Garlick's work was concerned with the relationship between all Australian universities, whether rural or metropolitan, and their respective regional economies, and sought to identify good collaborative practice in university's engagements with their regions. Traditionally the institution's contribution to the surrounding region was measured in terms of economic stimulus through enlarged employment, associated spending, extended cultural activities, and some community access to campus facilities. A number of institutions however are beginning to move beyond this "local largesse" approach towards a more strategic, systematic and pervasive engagement with their region for mutual benefit.

Importantly, the university may assume a totally involved approach with the regional community it is in by taking on community leadership responsibilities that embrace the region's strategic economic direction as part of its own strategic priorities. At this level the university and the community pursue a whole of institution/whole of community partnership approach to their respective economic futures, rather than a sector by sector approach, that embodies characteristics of a learning region.

Using extended analysis of public access materials, questionnaires to all universities, and six case study workshops, the project found that while there was an increasing will on the part of universities and some evidence of good practice in a number of university connections with their regions, there were a number of impediments at government policy, university management and community levels which were holding back the progress and strengthening of closer relationships. At present, there was no consistent or concerted effort that could yet be characterised as whole of institution and whole of community approach.

Recommendations to government included proposed changes to the formula criteria on which operating grants to universities are based, and changes to specific-purpose and grant programmes targeted at universities or to enhance general economic competitiveness. Regional communities were encouraged to better articulate the economic and developmental objectives which they wish the university to creatively engage with, and universities were urged to provide a clearer point of entry for the regional community into the university, to encourage, strengthen and reward greater staff involvement in regional initiatives, and to develop a long-term strategy in co-operation with regional leaders to pursue a learning region approach to economic competitiveness.

Britain

The current British HE system incorporates several distinct rounds of growth starting with the establishment of the ancient universities of Oxford and Cambridge in the twelfth and thirteenth centuries; the civic, red-brick universities of the late nineteenth century based in the major industrial cities such as Manchester, Leeds and Bristol; "new" universities prompted by the Robins Report of 1960s often located on green-field campuses; and, most recently, the former local authority controlled polytechnics which gained university status in 1992. In this year, a unified higher education sector was created in Britain and the number of institutions designated as universities nearly doubled to over 100. Within this new system most institutions have also seen massive expansion, as participation rates in higher education rose from 20% to 30% over a four-year period in the early 1990s. Accompanying this growth in numbers of institutions and students has been a reduction in the unit of resources, a shift to competitive allocation of block grants for research based on research quality assessment, and an increasing diversity of the character of institutions. As a result, stratification within the system continues with the "new" university sector (the former polytechnics) being outperformed by the "old" university sector (the rest) in recent government teaching and research assessments.

The development of the British higher education sector has not been greatly influenced by regional needs. However, more recently, a regional agenda has entered higher education as universities have been seen as important resources for disadvantaged regions, where levels of educational achievement and workforce skills tend to be poor. A number of explicit policy mechanisms have promoted greater university-regional engagement. Firstly, the expansion which occurred under the 1992 Further and Higher Education Act created a number of self-consciously local and regional universities from the old local authority owned polytechnics. Many were multi-sited and established outreach campuses in rural parts of Britain such as Cumbria and Devon.

Secondly, the contribution which universities can make to regional development was recognised by the National Committee of Inquiry into Higher Education (1997) (the Dearing Report) which devoted a chapter to the "Local and regional role of higher education" (Chapter 12), a supporting report (Report 9) and a number of specific recommendations to the Higher Education Funding Council and the Department for Education and Employment aimed at enhancing this role. This acknowledgement was timely as it provided an opportunity to exploit the emerging regional governance and devolution agenda in Britain.

The Dearing Report stated that one of the four main purposes of higher education is "to serve the needs of an adaptable, sustainable, knowledge-based economy at local, regional and national levels" (paragraph 5.11). The report continued by stating that: "Regional and local engagement should be a clear element in the role of higher education over the next 20 years. Each institution should be clear about its mission in relation to local communities and regions as part of the compact that we advocate between higher education and society." The report recognised that universities had a local and regional role to play in several areas such as research and consultancy, attracting inward investment, meeting labour market and skills needs, supporting lifelong learning and engaging in cultural and community development and stated that:

"In our view, the scope and need for collaboration will increase in future. It will derive strongly from the extended use of information and communication technology and from a stronger emphasis on the local and regional role of institutions. The framework for higher education qualifications will prompt dialogue about standards and the accumulation and transferability of credits at different levels. Lifelong learning and wider participation in higher education will foster collaboration between further and higher education institutions. Pressure on funding will stimulate joint purchasing and sharing of resources." (paragraph 16.42)

However, the Dearing Report also observed that "The evidence from the United Kingdom suggests that the extent of the local and regional involvement of institutions is currently patchy, but that it needs to turn to active and systematic engagement" (paragraph 12.7). In the light of this need for greater attention to regionalism, the report recommended that:

- An Industrial Partnership Fund should be established immediately to attract matching fund from industry, and to contribute to regional economic development (recommendation 34).
- HEIs should be represented on the boards of the new Regional Development Agencies (RDAs) and that further education funding council regional committees should include a member from higher education (recommendation 36).
- That funding should continue to be available after April 1998, when the present provision from the Higher Education Regional Development Fund is due to cease, to support human capital projects which enable higher education to be responsive to the needs of local industry and commerce (recommendation 37).
- Higher education institutions and their representative bodies should examine, with representatives of industry, ways of giving firms, especially small and medium sized enterprises, easy and co-ordinated access to

information about higher education services in their area (recommendation 38).

- The government should consider establishing a modest fund to provide equity funding to institutions to support members of staff or students in taking forward business ideas developed in the institution, and to support the creation of incubator units (recommendation 39).
- Higher education institutions should establish more technology incubator units within or close to the institution, within which start-up companies can be fostered for a limited period until they are able to stand alone (recommendation 39).

These challenges have been picked up in policies emanating from various central government departments. For example, the Department for the Environment, Transport and the Regions' White Paper (DETR, 1997) outlines its plans to establish Regional Development Agencies (RDAs) in the English regions. The core functions of RDAs will be:

- Leadership in developing and implementing regional economic strategies.
- Social, physical and economic regeneration.
- Economic development and regeneration of rural areas.
- Taking a leading role on European Union Structural Funds.
- Regional co-ordination of inward investment.
- Providing advice to ministers on regional selective assistance.
- Business support, with the business links.
- The reclamation and/or preparation of sites.
- Facilitating investments.
- Marketing of the region as a business location.
- Promoting technology transfer.
- Improvements to the skills base of the region.

The White Paper states that "we want RDAs to engage FE and HE fully in the regional agenda and improve co-operation between these sectors ... and ... work with universities to enhance the exploitation of the university knowledge base" (DETR, 1997, paragraph 6.7). Similar connections are made in the recent Competitiveness White Paper from the Department for Trade and Industry, which is significantly subtitled *Building the Knowledge Driven Economy* (DTI, 1998), in the Department for Education and Employment's consultation paper on *The Learning Age* (DfEE, 1998*b*) and, most significantly, in relation to the guidance given by the Secretary of State for Education to the Higher Education Funding Council for England (HEFCE) following the Comprehensive Spending Review which has identified extra funding for the sector for the next three years. Figure A1 summarises the main lines of influence of government policy on the regional role of HEIs.

The point to note about Figure A.1 is that a university's engagement with its region is influenced by funding emanating from four sources – the Department for the Environment, Transport and the Regions (DETR), the Department for Trade and Industry (DTI), the Department for Education and Employment (DfEE) and the Higher Education Funding Council for England (HEFCE).

Figure A.1. **Main lines of influence on regional engagement by English universities**

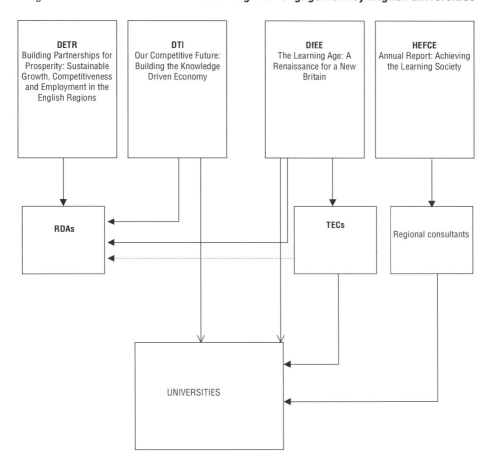

Dearing made great play about university representation on RDAs and this has come to pass with one vice-chancellor from each region sitting on the RDA board. Although the Committee of Vice-Chancellors and Principals (CVCP) presented the government with a slate of eight vice-chancellors for RDA board membership (one per region), only five were appointed. It also remains unclear how these individuals can relate back to all of the universities in their regions. In some regions there is an informal forum of vice-chancellors but none is constituted in a way that can collectively represent higher education. Indeed, HEFCE policy favours competition rather than collaboration amongst universities. While Dearing had a number of recommendations about collaboration these were expressed in a very limited way so as to "not discourage collaboration" (National Committee of Inquiry into Higher Education, 1997). Indeed, the chairman of the CVCP, in responding to a government announcement about funding for RDAs to support work with universities in shaping regional skills strategies has stated: "I do not think any of us would welcome giving the RDAs the role of imposing any local [higher education] planning structure". In short, regionalism in higher education policy is equated with planning and a reduction in institutional autonomy.

A further key point relating to RDAs is that they are essentially creatures of DETR with their core funding emerging from the Single Regeneration Budget (SRB) and staffed from English Partnerships and the Rural Development Commission. This implies an initial focus on the social and physical aspects of localised urban and rural development. While universities can contribute to this agenda, for example through research and policy guidance, these concerns are not central to the development of a regional knowledge economy.

In contrast, the DTIs priorities, as set out in *Building the Knowledge Driven Economy* (1998), have much to offer universities wishing to engage with industry and their region. DTI has hitherto lacked a regional delivery mechanism for its policies and clearly regards RDAs as providing this; but how this will evolve in practice remains unclear. Significantly, universities are given great emphasis as part of a national agenda which has an explicit regional dimension. Thus, in the foreword, the Secretary of State for Trade and Industry, challenges business "to turn into commercial success the technological knowledge in our universities... to form collective partnership with suppliers, customers, schools and universities to build networks and clusters of excellence to win competitive advantage". He promises to "reward universities for strategies and activities that enhance interaction with business ... and... encourage the development of entrepreneurship and skills especially amongst school pupils, students and university researchers".

The DTI White Paper itself makes much of collaboration, stating in the executive summary that "successful business depends upon strong teamwork – with suppliers, customers, joint venture partners and between managers and employees". It clearly sees a regional dimension to the agenda: "The government will act as a catalyst to promote creative collaboration between businesses and within regions". To support entrepreneurship, the White Paper announces the extension of the Young Enterprise Scheme into HE and the funding of eight new enterprise centres in universities which will equip scientists and engineers with entrepreneurship and business skills and develop the transfer and exploitation of knowledge and know-how. These centres will be paralleled by the University Challenge Fund established jointly by the treasury, the Wellcome Trust and Gatsby Foundation to provide seed funding to help selective universities around the country make the most of research funding through support for the early stages of commercial exploitation of new products and processes. To support regional innovation, RDAs are being asked to prepare regional innovation strategies. These will be backed by a new "Higher Education Reach Out Fund" jointly sponsored by DTI, DfEE and HEFCE to "reward universities for strategies and activities which enhance interaction with business, promote technology and knowledge transfer, strengthen higher level skills development and improve student employability and help recognise the importance of university interaction with business alongside education and research". There will also be an extension of the national Faraday

Partnership Scheme linking universities and small businesses, an expansion of the Teaching Company Scheme and a new regional Foresight Programme.

Significantly, the DTI White Paper does address skills issues within the domain of the DfEE and recognises the regional dimension to this topic. Funds are to be allocated to RDAs to "identify the key skills gap affecting regional economic development and to set out plans for addressing these covering *all* the main sectors of education and training". In its benchmarking of the United Kingdom against other industrial nations, the White Paper highlights the poor performance of the United Kingdom in *intermediate* and technical skills. Consequently, the priority for expansion is in further and not higher education.

This priority chimes in with DfEE's concerns about expanding access to further and higher education. Thus, of the 61 000 extra student numbers to be available by 2001, 20 000 and 15 000 respectively are to be in part- and full-time sub-degree programmes and only 6 000 in full-time first degree programmes. Furthermore, within the traditional student body, HEFCE will provide universities with a premium within its funding formula which recognises success in recruitment of students from disadvantaged backgrounds (defined in terms of postcode geography). Further funds will be provided by HEFCE to encourage links with schools and FE and which facilitate student progression. University performance will also be assessed on the output side in terms of employment outcomes. Finally, in its guidance to HEFCE, DfEE asks universities to:

> "Refocus their outreach programmes. These should cover the regeneration of the economy in the specific local economy within which the university has a legitimate interest; partnership work with adult education and other providers offering access to those groups who have traditionally been disadvantaged in relation to lifelong learning; and a contribution in terms of the role education can play in making expertise and facilities available to overcome exclusion and social isolation. "

HEFCE has already introduced a series of schemes outwith its core funding of teaching and research under which universities can bid for additional resources to meet the objectives laid down by the government and in so doing maintain the Funding Council's position as a funding and not a planning body. Nevertheless, through the appointment of consultants with responsibility for each region who will work with RDAs and TECs and their counterparts in the FEFC (Further Education Funding Council), an element of regional steering of higher education is inevitable.

As to TECs there is an on-going review of their relationship to RDAs, the outcome of which will affect the links TECs currently have with universities. Because of the variable quality and interests of TECs, the nature of this relationship has hitherto contributed to the "patchy" engagement of universities with their local communities as noted by the National Committee of Inquiry into Higher Education (1997). It is also partly attributable to the fact that TECs are primarily organisations delivering national policy at a local level with their funding clearly related to national numerical output targets, principally in relation to lower level skills. Some TECs have launched significant schemes to enhance graduate retention within their area, but the fact that TECs operate on a highly localised, as distinct from a regional or sub-regional, basis severely constrains the possibility of engagement in a significant way with the higher level skills agenda relevant to universities. If the experience of TECs is repeated in RDAs – that is an emphasis on the delivery of national programmes and strict adherence to territorial boundaries – this could severely hamper the development of a learning system which includes regional engagement by universities, particularly by those universities whose sphere of influence does not coincide with an administrative geography.

Taken together, these initiatives have major implications in terms of how universities relate to the regions in which they are located. While RDAs are seen to have a significant role to play, they will essentially be executive arms of national government, implementing national policy at a regional level. Funds for those programmes which are administered directly by RDAs will be allocated as has been the case with TECs on a *per capita* basis using national criteria and not on the basis of regional needs. To compensate less prosperous regions such as the North-East of England, there needs to be an equivalent to the treasury formula which has hitherto been used to top-up national programmes in Scotland. In addition, there will be individual departmental and HEFCE programmes which deal directly with universities without regard to RDAs. In short, there is no intention to introduce a regional dimension to the support of HE within England.

The key point here is that HE in England has evolved as a national system, but is now being required to adjust to meet a new set of regional needs with no specific funds to enable this adjustment to take place. A few indicators of uneven development in the knowledge economy, focusing upon the North-East of England, should suffice to emphasise the problem. In terms of learning and teaching, and compared to a national average of 100, the index of the working population with a degree in the North-East is 71, and employees with no qualification 127; only 4.8% of schools had a web page in 1997 compared to 23% in the South-East; 12.6% of households owned a computer compared to 29% in the South-East and 80% had telephones compared to 96% in the South-East.

These statistics need to be set alongside data on the flow of students into higher education and subsequently into the labour market. University admissions statistics reveal a clear North-South divide with lower participation in higher education in the Northern region and students from this region more likely to attend a local university. For example, 46.0% of applicants to universities in the Northern region live in the region, compared to 33.8% in the case of South-East universities. There is a strong South to North transfer of undergraduates because of the limited supply of places in those regions with the highest demand and the ability of the more relatively prosperous students to live away from home. Not surprisingly, it is the former polytechnics which recruit most local students – in the North-East 53.3% of the graduates from the post-1992 universities come from homes in the region compared to 24.3% for graduates from the older universities. It is these local graduates who are most likely to find themselves unemployed six months after graduation – unemployment rates for non-local students for old universities in the region is 6.9% compared with 12.9% for local students graduating from the former polytechnics (DfEE, 1998*a*).

Turning to university links with regional industry, universities in the North face the problem of limited local demand given the concentration of R-D and knowledge based industries in the South-East. Thus, in the North-East in 1995, business expenditure on R-D as a percentage of regional GDP was only 0.9% compared to 3% in the eastern region; and only 4.7% of employment was in knowledge intensive business services compared to 9.1% in the South-East. Furthermore, the North-East figure for knowledge intensive services has fallen by 15% since 1991, whilst for the South-East it has grown by 20% (CURDS, 1997). These figures confirm the findings of a recent analysis of university and academic links which reveals that universities in the south-east and eastern regions have both stronger global *and* local contract linkages than those elsewhere in the country (Howells *et al.*, 1998). Thus, universities in these core regions receive 60% of the total research grant and contract income awarded to UK universities, but more significantly, they receive 77% of all research and contract income from overseas sources (outside the EU); they also report that 29% of their research income is from firms with under 500 employees compared with an average of 17% for universities elsewhere.

In summary, universities outside the South face a more uphill struggle in fulfilling the aspirations for the sector as set out in the White Paper on Competitiveness. Regions like the North-East are not only disadvantaged in the knowledge economy, the historic pattern of student recruitment and graduate placement in the labour market does not appear to have reduced that disadvantage.

This discussion has highlighted the fact that different parts of central government have an influence on the regional role of universities, although the primary responsibility for funding lies with DfEE. Through the research and intelligence activities of HEFCE and DfEE, a clearer picture is beginning to emerge of the geography of higher education in England but much more work is required to provide a consistent background to regional policy making. A fundamental task covering both FE and HE is to establish what courses are taught where, the home origins of students and where students enter the labour market. Such analyses need to be benchmarked against regional data on participation in higher education and industrial and occupational structure to identify areas of under and over provision. A particular concern of this mapping task will be to identify the steps between different levels of the education system – schools, further/vocational education, higher education, postgraduate institutions – in order to assess how far the regional pattern of provision assists/inhibits access and progress of students. In short, geographical analysis should highlight the fact that lifelong learning is an agenda that should be responsive to the needs of people in places.

Similar work needs to be done on the geography of industry interactions building upon the work of Howells *et al.* (1998) to embrace the teaching and learning aspects as well as research and consultancy contracts (*e.g.* student placements). At an inter-ministerial level, as well as within universities, the links between learning and teaching and technology transfer need to be pursued between the DTI and the DfEE.

The key question is how this information should guide funding mechanisms. The current process is to establish national competitions for earmarked funding designed to address particular issues such as access, fostering academic entrepreneurship or supporting new business ventures. The pattern of winners and losers from such competitions may or may not address questions of uneven development within the knowledge economy. Furthermore, this process imposes a high overhead on university management which is required to respond to successive invitations to tender. There are also problems of sustainability if funding runs out before the activity becomes "mainstreamed". Although competitive schemes do promote innovation, there is a strong case for some block funding for university to enable them to sustain a programme of regionally relevant activity tailored to the institution's own mission and to local circumstances. This might take the form of a rolling contract between the university and the funding body (which might be either HEFCE or the RDA) and against which performance could be monitored. A key dimension of such performance is likely to be evidence of partnership building within the regional education sector and with other public and private agencies.

Scotland represents a notable example of how collaboration can be promoted between higher education institutions. As the Report of the Scottish Committee observed:

"The Scottish Higher Education System is a good size for sharing staff, facilities and equipment on a regional basis... There is already a great deal of collaboration either at the institutions' own behest or through SHEFC funded initiatives."

In particular, the Higher Education Funding Council of Scotland has established the Regional Strategic Initiatives Fund (RSIF) to meet the costs of establishing collaborative arrangements and projects which without initial funding might not occur. RSIF had an initial budget of £5 million which funded 62 projects over four designated regions in Scotland. Projects involved fostering collaboration in the areas of teaching, research and administration.

However, faced by resistance from universities, the Dearing Report has been unable to deliver policy changes which would significantly shift higher education towards regionalism. There is little support from individual HEIs in Britain to create a nationally planned system of HE at the regional level. This reluctance stems, in part, from an acknowledgement that there is a great variety between regional contexts within England and that each HEI must develop strategies appropriate to its own context. There are also marked differences in the capacity for collaboration, the strength of identities and the existence of regional actors between British regions. In the context of England, this is confounded by disagreements concerning the definition of regions. In particular, there are many divergences between the standard planning regions of England and definition of regions employed by each HEI.

Most HEIs believe that a centrally planned system would make them unresponsive to regional needs, opportunities and constraints. This anti-planning sentiment is also mirrored in the attitude towards HE-FE links, where voluntarily negotiated arrangements are preferred over nationally imposed links between the two sectors. In sum, whilst making a great play of the importance of the regional dimension, the Dearing Committee's recommendations concerning regionalism were limited in scale and scope. In particular, insufficient attention was paid to the provision of funds to finance regionally-based activity within HEIs.

However, one area of progress towards regional planning in HE is the establishment of regional advisors by the Higher Education Funding Council of England (HEFCE) which, ideally, would work closely with the proposed Regional Development Agencies. Yet, there is almost universal opposition to the idea that such new posts would signify the move to a regionally-based allocation of funds or student quota system in Britain. It is likely that the agenda outlined by the Dearing Report will allow regionalism within the HE sector to develop due to the benefits accrued from collaborative teaching and research, contributing to regional human resources development and skills needs, and, more generally, enhancing the economic, social and cultural life of the region. Moreover, the emergence of a new tier of regionally embedded development agencies in Britain will give added momentum to the regional role of HEIs as outlined by Dearing.

A further driver to regionalism in British higher education stems from the government commitment to further widen access to post-compulsory education, by providing an additional 500 000 places in further and higher education by 2002. In its Green Paper, "The Learning Age", the government expects that 60% of school leavers would experience higher education at some point in their lives. This move to a more mass education system signifies the erosion of the particularity of the United Kingdom, in which the majority of university students studied away from home assisted by government-paid fees for the first degree, and maintenance subsidies for the poor. With the introduction of student contributions to tuition fees and the erosion of maintenance grants, coupled with greater numbers entering higher education, and many more mature students with non-traditional entry qualifications entering HE, a much greater proportion are attending their local university. This signifies a changing relationship between the state, students and HEIs, in that the financial cost of studying at an HEI is being passed from the state to the individual.

HEI expansion is to be complemented in Britain by the University for Industry (UfI) which proposes to be a major mechanism for the promotion of a culture of lifelong learning in Britain, especially in terms of meeting the needs of SMEs.

All of these developments are having effects on the nature of the learning process, the nature of the curriculum, the flows of young people between regions, and the role of HEIs as social escalators. The full consequences of this localisation of learning are yet to be determined but it may be expected that some of these changes will affect the nature and character of regional skill bases and the networks and culture for innovation in the regions.

Finland

This section discusses recent developments in the higher education system in Eastern Finland which provide us with an interesting study of the ways in which HEIs have been mobilised as tools of regional development. The Finnish higher education system has its origins in the seventeenth century and currently consists of 20 public universities, ten of which are multi-faculty, six specialist institutions and four universities of arts. The University of Helsinki is by far the largest university with over 33 000 students out of a total of nearly 143 000 HE students in Finland. As part of the Nordic welfare state tradition, tuition fees are not charged to students.

In addition to the universities, in 1991, nine permanent and 20 experimental polytechnic institutions (AMKs) were established through mergers and upgrading of existing specialised and vocational institutions. These institutions are, in large, teaching institutions and form a distinct part of the HE sector. The AMKs are locally or privately run and in many cases, local authorities have come together to form a private limited company to run the institution. As a result, they are regional by nature and offer a broad range of studies to meet the needs of local business and industry. It is estimated that by 2000, the system will be comprised of 30 permanent institutions. The university and non-university systems, then, have developed quite separately, but taken together, they aim to increase participation in tertiary education to 60-65%.

HE has a long history of involvement in regional development in Finland, in particular to disperse activity away from the south of the country. University education was restricted to the capital, Helsinki, until the first decade of the twentieth century, when its monopoly was broken and two universities were established in Turku. From this date, a number of successive rounds of growth in the 1950s, 1960s and 1970s expanded HE provision away from the core southern area of the country. For example, the University of Oulu was established in the mid 1950s to promote the development of the north of the country and during the 1960s and 1970s, the Finnish government established a regional network of universities as part of its far-reaching regionalisation policy. More specifically, the establishment of universities in northern and eastern provinces were directly aimed at accelerating the economic growth and cultural diversification of these sparsely populated and marginal regions and to integrate the whole of the Finnish national territory. This trend is also evident in the neighbouring countries of Norway and Sweden.

Centres for continuing education contained within each university enhance this regionalisation policy by expanding HE provision to wider groups. Over 200 000 students now take part in continuing or open and distance learning through the centres, much of which occurs in provincial outreach centres. The centres function to promote equality, but increasingly exist to generate income and, in the face of rising unemployment, match the skills of graduates with the needs of the economy. The centres have received substantial funds from EU structural funds and generate more than one third of the total income from all commercial services provided by universities in Finland. The Virtual Open University, a nation wide project, is also being developed by the government to extend participation.

In the context of Eastern Finland it was decided that HEIs would be used as a central element of regional development, but it was initially unclear as to what format the HEIs should take. The eventual outcome was to establish three specialist provincial centres instead of one large comprehensive university for the whole region. Three independent universities were established at Kuopio (specialising in medicine), Lappeenranta (technology and engineering), and Joensuu (education). In this sense, what emerged were three universities *in* Eastern Finland, not a university *of* Eastern Finland. Each of the universities had a degree of freedom to pursue their regional mission. In this context of specialised regional institutions, it is important to estimate the collective impact of all three institutions upon the region.

These universities, now established for some thirty years, face a changing regional context in a number of respects. Firstly, the universities have a new set of regional actors, such as the regional councils, with which to engage. Secondly, the establishment of the AMK higher education institutions which have strong regional affiliations raises a number of issues for universities with regard to their role as regional higher education providers. The centres for continuing education, which co-ordinate many of the regional links within each of the three universities play a key role in regional engagement in Eastern Finland and represent a useful model of how regional engagement might be mainstreamed into the management of universities. In particular, there is potential for the centres to work together with each other and regional stakeholders to develop Eastern Finland.

What have been the effects of the regionalisation of higher education on a region such as East Finland which has experienced depopulation and economic restructuring over the last few decades? Population decline has slowed in the region, which can only be partly ascribed to the establishment of these institutions. The three institutions had a more significant impact in terms of diminishing the gap between region enrolments and national enrolments in higher education. In particular, more people are staying in East Finland to study at one of the three institutions, rather than migrating to areas of concentration such as Helsinki. This retention of students is of significant economic and cultural benefit to this already marginal region. Further, the universities have contributed to "competence building" in East Finland by establishing skills, training and leadership.

One of the main conclusions from a recent review of the higher education system in Eastern Finland is that whilst many universities owe their foundation to impulses towards regionalism, they are now having to function in a vacuum with regard to government policy and mechanisms which further foster regionalism.

France

The structure of French higher education is complex and its specific characteristics can be difficult to grasp without sustained immersion in French culture and society. The French higher education sector has a number of distinctive features. At the post-compulsory level it is divided into Level V (BEP, CAP qualifications), Level IV (the highly symbolic *baccalauréat*), Level III (DUT, BTS) and Levels I and II (the licence degree and beyond). It has set ambitious standards for growth; for example, a target of 80% of the age cohort are to attain *baccalauréat* level education by 2000.

The higher education system is very fragmented and is comprised of institutions which vary considerably in terms of profile, size and status and cater for different clienteles from well-defined segments of French society (OECD, 1996). The initial objectives of the system is to renew the university and social elite without being over concerned about the future of other people who have already been through university and even today, the French educational system basically trains more wage-earners than entrepreneurs. The system includes many types of institutions, including both the old traditional universities and the "university colleges" established in the 1960s in medium sized towns without a university tradition; *grandes écoles* (higher professional schools) and their "preparatory classes"; polytechnics divided between upper classes (postsecondary) of technical grammar schools and university institutes of technology (IUT), both delivering a kind of "associate degree" two years after the leaving certificate; and other tertiary establishments (specialising in specific subjects such as arts, architecture, agriculture, social work). Note, in addition, that, within specific agreements, much of the research is done or coordinated by the National Centre for Scientific Research (CNRS) which is a state institution not controlled by universities.

Further, there are important distinctions between short-cycle and long-cycle courses and selective and non-selective entry routes to higher education. Institutions offering short-cycle higher education include the university institutes of technology (IUT) established in 1966, the post-baccalauréat lycée classes (advanced technician sections known as STS), and specialist vocational institutions which account for approximately 25% of the 2 million higher education students in France. Entrance to these short courses is often more selective and competitive than for university places. Long-cycle higher education is provided in 86 comprehensive universities which are based upon the principle of free admission for students with a high-school degree (*baccalauréat*). A minority of 5% of students gain entrance to the highly selective and prestigious *grandes écoles* which are specialised institutes of higher education focusing on areas such as engineering or business. The most prestigious amongst these is the *école polytechnique* established at the end of the 18th century. It is now regarded as the most important technical school in the country.

The French system of higher education is also distinctive in that it is more *local/regional* than in countries such as the United Kingdom. High levels of students attend home universities and up to two-thirds of graduates are retained in the region in which they studied. However, there are inter-regional variations which reflect the size and structure of the university sector and the economic fabric of the region. For example, the Ile-de-France attracts many students from other regions and, due to its prosperity, also retains over 80% of its graduates whilst regions such as Languedoc-Roussillon generally lack the ability both to attract students and to retain graduates.

Further, a particularly marked feature of the French higher education system, and indeed French society more generally, has been the high degree of centralisation and the pre-eminent role of the state (OECD, 1996). Education is seen as one of the main mechanisms through which a unified French society based around republican values is maintained. However, there have been moves towards decentralisation in France over the last 20 years which have also extended to the education system and the universities. In particular, universities were given greater autonomy under the Savary reforms of 1984 which reduced the influence of the central state. This process of increased autonomy for universities began earlier, in 1968, under the Edgar Faure reforms which changed higher education profoundly. In 1968, the subject-based faculties which composed universities until then, were replaced by teaching and research units regrouped into autonomous, multidisciplinary universities in cities with only one university. In other cities, several universities were established around main disciplinary poles rather than as truly multidisciplinary universities. These new establishments had the power to determine research and teaching agendas, but decisions over curriculum remained at the national level. These reforms also attempted to increase occupational training within universities and reflected the wider assault on elitist models of university education which occurred in many parts of the world during this period.

A number of themes can be identified which are promoting a regional agenda in the French HE system. In a centralised country such as France where university development has always been seen as a matter of national policy, the decentralisation and regionalisation of higher education reflects a response to concerns about inter-regional disparities rather than a proactive response to building regional learning systems. In spite of the strengths of a centralised university system such as the ability to effectively and rapidly implement widespread reforms, moves towards decentralisation have occurred due to the inertia, bureaucracy and susceptibility to short-term political agendas within the system. One trend in France has been the need to respond to the massification of higher education by building new universities in areas which were lagging behind in terms of enrolments. In this context, central authorities have created universities of a regional nature, offering new curricula supposed to back local socio-economic development in areas such as Valenciennes, Le Havre, La Rochelle, Troyes and Belfort.

For administrative purposes, the education system is divided into 28 *académies*, each one headed by a rector who is the university chancellor and is the interlocutor for central ministers and regional authorities. The *académies* have experienced a transfer of power from the centre and no longer function as executors of orders received from central government. Moreover, local authorities have also received greater decision making powers and resources over vocational education and training. However, the dead weight of a long tradition of centralism still exists and, in spite of this decentralisation and greater institutional autonomy, the state retains power over funding, staff recruitment, curricula design, and collating university grades through the Ministry of Higher Education and Research.

The regional policy of higher education is framed within what is now an overall six-year contractual plan between the state and each region which mainly concerns investment in capital and equipment shared between the state and the local authorities. These investments are supposed to respond to a number of key developmental objectives in the region. Recently, a new procedure has accompanied the preparation of such objectives in which regional schemes of higher education and research guide the investment proposals for higher education.

In 1988, a charter for the development of the scientific and technological research and of higher education defined a series of co-ordinated actions between the state, the establishments, the local authorities and industry. It was concretised in 1990 by the launching of the "University 2000 project", a long-term plan for the concerted development of training nation-wide and to ensure the coherence of national and institutional policy. The expenses of the project are usually shared between the state (50%), the region (25%) and the other local authorities (25%). Recently, the costs were shared one third each in certain regions, proving the great interest of local authorities in developing their higher education infrastructure.

Further, the regional objectives of each university are embedded in a formal university working plan. Such a plan is one of the bases for the four-year contractual plan framing the relationships between the university and the state. Each higher education establishment has already been evaluated at least once by the National Committee of Evaluation which has now started to review specific sites where several higher education institutions co-exist. A first review concerned the Lyon metropolitan area and referred to the regional impact of these institutions.

Universities are also being encouraged to expand information and orientation services and to set up units to monitor students entering the regional labour market. Regional authorities, in partnership with the rector of the corresponding academies, are obliged to draw up training forecasts to outline training needs which are used to create a framework for the growth or contraction of training establishments. Moreover, almost all regions have signed an agreement with central government to administer continuing vocational training within which regional councils play a pivotal role.

There are still concerns within the French higher education sector with regard to the longer term consequences of decentralisation. Greater decentralisation to the regional level requires greater national co-ordination to ensure that different areas adhere to one vision. In this sense, in an increasingly decentralised and complex education system there is a pressing need for greater strategic planning and steering at the national level (*pilotage*) to determine the relationship between the constituent parts. The introduction of such strategic planning requires action to be taken in four simultaneous directions: at the level of society; in the educational system; at the regional level; and by specialists in the sector (OECD, 1996). Thus, the French system of education at all levels has become interested in steering as a response to pressures such as changing patterns of demand, technological progress and wider moves towards decentralisation within French society. This steering has created more room for local initiative. Yet the question of how to ensure system-wide coherence remains (OECD, 1996).

The system of the *grandes écoles* has long been disassociated from the higher education system of universities, declaring its autonomy in terms of its professional orientation and its links with companies, its regional and local implication in the dynamic of innovation and the fostering of development. Indeed, the *grandes écoles* became the initial springboard for greater entrepreneurialism through the creation of suitable interfaces for pinpointing and responding to the requirements of industrialists, the initial aim being to offer higher quality education.

Besides the decisions taken in the *grandes écoles* in France, it should also be mentioned that this professionalising approach between the higher education and the labour market has been made evident in recent years basically via the initiatives developed in the university institutes of technology (IUT) and professional institutes (IUP), which for some time now have been called upon to develop alternative studies that require *stages* and in-company research projects. Long before that, the technical *lycées* had already developed links and structures in their post-bachelor's degree sections which make it possible to manage the training/industry interface in a lasting way.

These initiatives, amongst others, have been responsible for a growth in vocationally oriented education over the last 20 years. This expansion represented an overhaul of the declining system of vocational training in France and an attempt to create an effective and socially accepted vocational system alongside the well established system of higher education. The success of the system relies upon creating autonomous institutions for vocational training and education. In this sense, a number of technological and vocational training options have been created. Qualifications such as the CAP and BEP are undertaken in vocational *lycées*, which prepare students for the vocational *baccalauréat*. This qualification was introduced in the 1980s to allow access to higher education combined with preparing students for entry into the labour market in skilled technical occupations. However, it has proved difficult to maintain the distinctiveness of vocational qualifications as qualifications such as the "vocational baccalauréat" have become associated with mainstream rather than vocational educational institutions. More specifically, the IUTs have moved from their original higher vocational role to be regarded as efficient institutions for general *baccalauréat* holders to enter the job market, or to access higher education while avoiding the traditional first cycle of university where the failure rate is very high. Higher vocational (*bac* + 2 qualifications such as the BTS, conducted in post-*baccalauréat* classes, and DUT, conducted in IUTs) training has also grown over the last 20 years. It supplies highly qualified intermediate technical and business graduates; the latter, as well as other students, may go on to a higher level and obtain a *bac* + 4 qualification in vocationally-oriented university institutes (IUP).

With this growth of vocational education, the universities have a role to play in vocational training at the regional level. In particular, the Faure Laws of 1968 stated that universities "must meet the nation's needs by providing managers in all areas and by taking part in the social and economic development of each region". Universities were granted greater autonomy to enable them to achieve such goals and to reduce the gap between them and the *grandes écoles*. As a result, a number of occupationally-oriented degrees have emerged in the university system in the post-1968 period. These reforms mark a significant step towards French universities playing a role in meeting social and economic needs. HEIs also have an increasing role to play in continuing education provision, especially since the Law of 1971 which gave all employees a right to paid training leave.

Abbreviations:

BEP	Brevet d'enseignement professionnel
CAP	Certificat d'aptitude professionnelle
IUT	Institut universitaire de technologie
DUT	Diplôme universitaire de technologie
BTS	Brevet de technicien supérieur

Spain

Introduction

The speed with which Spanish society has developed during the last 20 years, after the fall of the regime of Franco and the beginning of democratic rule, has no equal in Europe and this is reflected in the education reforms which have been undertaken at all levels and in particular in the development of higher education, which was considered by OECD (1986) "more spectacular than in any other OECD country". For example, in 1976, public expenditure on higher education was much lower than the European average while only fifteen years later, in 1991, it was more than four times higher. This increase in expenditure is impressive in the light of the economic crisis of the 1980s.

The general growth of higher education in Spain, and particularly in Catalonia, is a result of increasing demand, which was inhibited under Franco: the number of university students has quadrupled since 1970. After a period of rapid expansion, the Spanish university system now faces a new and more difficult challenge in terms of improving the efficiency, effectiveness and quality of the system. These issues are now influencing university staff and students, as well as public opinion, all actors who could be resistant to innovations which affect more than just the institutional and financial framework of higher education.

Such growth has changed the relationship between the university and non-university sectors of higher education. Until recently it could be asserted that there was only a university sector in Spain and that the non-university sector of higher education represented a minimal part of the system, being composed of specialist schools (languages, military, music, etc.). However the development plans of the Ministry of Education and Culture (MEC) forecast an increase in public spending for the non-university sector by the year 2004 which would be twice as large as that for the university sector. In parallel to the universities, different institutions, such as the higher technical schools (*escuelas técnicas superiores*) or university schools (*escuelas universitarias*), are growing in number and in importance. The trend in Spanish higher education reforms is towards the integration of these institutions within the university system. Many teacher-training colleges (*escuelas de formación del profesorado de EGB*) have already been merged with universities. However, recently it appears that the non-university institutions are more capable than the universities of responding to professional and social needs.

Higher education in Spain is conducted almost entirely under the auspices of the universities. Only a few courses in higher education are studied in institutions not affiliated to universities. Such institutions are the responsibility of specific central government ministries or of the *Communidades Autónomas*. The latter applies to Catalonia, whose government gained full responsibility in higher education, although not in research, in 1985. However, the basic laws regarding university education are still a responsibility of the central government and, to the present, the Catalan government has not yet developed a differentiated model of higher education provision.

Non-university higher education consists of courses leading to the qualification of *Técnico en Empresas y Actividades Turísticas* (tourism and related activities) which are taught in *escuelas* under the responsibility of the Ministry of Transport and Communications and advanced art studies, for which the Ministry of Education and Science is responsible (dramatic art and dance, singing, and academies of music).

The university system in Spain consists of public universities, private universities and universities belonging to the Catholic Church under a special agreement with the Vatican State; on the whole public universities cater for the majority of the student population both in Spain and particularly in Catalonia. In principle, all universities, which must be recognised by law, are full curriculum universities which provide, according to their circumstances, courses in the various fields of knowledge (experimental science, social science and law, the humanities, medicine, engineering and technology, etc.) and at all levels (1st, 2nd and 3rd cycle or *doctorado*). However, three of them, known as *universidades politécnicas* specialise in technical areas such as engineering and technology. These subjects are also studied in the other universities alongside other branches of science and the humanities.

All state universities in Spain organise their teaching in accordance with a common basic structure consisting of: *facultades universitarias, escuelas técnicas superiores, escuelas universitarias* and *colegios universitarios*. These institutions are responsible for organising and administering the courses leading to the various academic degrees. The courses vary in length and can be long or short. *Facultades universitarias* and *escuelas técnicas superiores* organise long courses lasting five or six years. The former offer science and the humanities whilst the latter teach only technology, engineering and architecture. The *escuelas universitarias* are institutions responsible for short courses lasting three years. These are of an applied or vocational nature, and are similar in structure to first cycle university courses. The *colegios universitarios* offer only the first three years of university studies for students who intend to continue their university course in the related university faculty. They were set up to decentralise university teaching and make it more widely available.

In addition, there are *escuelas universitarias* (and, in a few cases, *facultades* as well) which, although not legally a part of a university institution because they are privately owned, are nevertheless linked ("assigned") to the university. Such *escuelas* or *facultades* differ in having their own administrative rules and entrance fees, but have the same educational administration as their sponsoring university.

Reform acts

The first attempt at university reform was the 1970 Act which aimed at providing more autonomy for universities, but prescribed very tightly how universities should be organised and how the courses should be planned and taught. Fifteen years later many provisions of this act had still not been implemented and many of the new institutions which were created during this period, both universities and colleges, resembled the traditional universities in their structure and teaching.

In contrast, the new University Reform Act (LRU – *Ley de reforma universitaria*) approved in 1983 gave birth to a ten-year reform process which was completed in 1992 and which has given and is still giving new shape and new characteristics to the higher education system in Spain. The LRU was a large framework law which gave guidelines and responsibility to the government to enact the necessary measures by royal decrees. Its basic principles were the priority of the public university, the promotion and regulation of a system of separate competitive institutions and a more powerful departmental structure.

One of the most important changes at the institutional level, was the transfer of power of legislation in this area to the regional level of the *Comunidades Autónomas*. From 1985 to 1987, Cataluña, País Vasco, Comunidad Valenciana, Andalucía, Canarias and Galicia were given authority and regulatory power over higher education: they can now establish new universities or higher education institutions according to national plans and guidelines. The reform also created a National Council of Universities (*Consejo de Universidades*) in 1985 with the task of laying down and monitoring general aspects of university life, in relation to teaching and research. In the same year another important national body was established, the *Consejo Social de Universidades*, which deals with all the financial and administrative aspects of university life. This council is composed of representatives from all the universities and from the most important economic and social organisations within Spanish society. According to the LRU and the royal decrees on departmental organisation and on university curricula, each institution defines and approves its own statutes and curricula, under the supervision of the regional authorities. The legal validity of university degrees all over the country is still guaranteed by the state, but the individual institution may deliver a number of different certificates and titles, which were recognised by several royal decrees between November 1990 to October 1991.

The reform itself and the subsequent financial measures aimed year by year to change the proportion of the number of students who graduated at different levels. Previously Spanish universities produced mainly graduates of a relatively long cycle (*licenciatura*). Because of a number of issues to be discussed later, but primarily due to the changing demands of the job market, several measures have been taken to increase the number and the variety of short cycle courses (*diplomatura*) and therefore the number of students qualified at intermediate level.

The LRU also represented a step forward in the democratisation of university management. The heads of departments, faculties and universities are all elected with the result that Spanish universities have very advanced democratic and participatory structures. However, the power within higher education institutions is tightly linked to the selection, appointment, status and career of the teaching staff. From the royal decree of 1985 until the recent proposal (1994) of a *Ley de actualización de la Ley de reforma universitaria*, a long and difficult process of transformation of the selection criteria for the appointment of professors has been undertaken. The traditional method of internal appointment by each university is seen as "endogamic": between June 1991 and January 1992, 91% of appointments were filled internally and cases of highly qualified experts rejected in favour of internal poorly qualified candidates were not unusual. Finally, the reform has started a long and difficult process of quality control over higher education which has already progressed through a number of phases and which is leading to a more evaluative state, as opposed to the initial model of a state provider.

Autonomy and control

The number of private higher education institutions, both university and non university, has grown rapidly since 1991 as a result of several aspects of the university reform, which have encouraged the creation of new state and private higher education institutions. The most important aspect of the long standing reformation process is autonomy. This allows any higher education institution to establish its own statutes; elect, appoint and dismiss its own governing and administrative bodies; prepare, approve and manage the distribution of its resources and its estates; employ, transfer, select and train its own personnel; deliver titles and degrees; and establish external relations with other higher education institutions and cultural or scientific organisations, in Spain and abroad.

A framework for the autonomous institutions is, of course, established by law and royal decrees and control over adherence to the established guidelines is exercised, at a national level, by the two previously mentioned councils: *Consejo de Universidades* and *Consejo Social de Universidades*, and at community level, by different bodies set up by the Comunidades Autónomas. The councils act as buffers between the public administration and the higher education institutions and are usually composed of rectors or presidents of the institutions concerned and representatives of the national and community administration.

The debate about the positive and negative aspects of autonomy is still very heated, although traditionally the Catalan government has supported public universities in their quest for increased autonomy. Autonomy, self-government and decentralisation under community control, are seen as positive in that diversity is rewarded and encouraged, and because of the closer links between higher education and society in responding to local needs. Negative aspects are the risk of "endogamy" or self-referential quality and the inevitable inequalities between small and large or poor and wealthy institutions. Because of this autonomy, a fundamental change in the organisation of teaching, a new financing system and measures for quality control have become crucial for the success or the failure of the whole reformation process.

Financing of institutions

Spanish state universities are mainly financed by the regional administrations: in 1993 more than 80% of the budget came from public funding and around 12% from student fees. At the beginning of the reform process, no explicit mechanism existed to allocate funds among the universities. The allocations were made on the basis of direct negotiations between the representatives of the administration and of the universities, and negotiations between the communities and the state.

141

On the basis of a trial model developed at the University of Valencia, which allocated funds according to a set of indicators, in 1995, the national *Consejo de Universidades* issued new funding proposals within a report on financing the university (*Informe sobre financiación de la universidad*). This aimed to establish a rational framework for financing public universities together with a financial mechanism to promote quality. The report was based on the following general assumptions: the majority of state university funding must remain public; self-financing through student fees and external contracts must be increased; part of the funding for universities should be based on competitive, quality-related criteria; relative capital expenditure was predicted to decrease with the end of the period of demographic expansion; and current expenditure for goods and services should increase more than staffing costs.

The proposals would not affect the principle that money is now given to universities on a lump sum basis so that institutions are free to allocate the received funds to different budget lines as they wish. However it is clear that, if the model was adopted, all the incentives and additional private and public resources above the basic funding would be allocated on a competitive basis, according to the achievement of the proposed aims, thereby rewarding or punishing the policy of each institution. The consequence of the new autonomy together with the increasing size of many universities is that internal allocation of resources has led to serious imbalances inside the institutions.

Quality control and evaluation

The aim of stimulating good quality universities was one of the priorities of the reform. From the beginning the following main areas were and still are a focus of attention: teaching, research and management. The first attempt to set up mechanisms for quality assessment was undertaken in 1990 by the Ministry of Education with no discussion or testing of the assessment criteria. This assessment process focused on the tenured academic staff: for each period in which they were given a positive assessment, they received a small increase in salary.

This initial experiment failed to achieve reasonable results. Because of the lack of reliable standards for the assessment of the teaching work, all staff were positively assessed, and the system has become a way of rewarding seniority without improving teaching. Some more rigorous procedures were established for the assessment of research activity: a national committee was established that brought together experts from the main scientific fields, and some tenured staff were evaluated negatively. However, there was controversy about the lack of scientific accuracy of the criteria used to assess research. It could be argued that such evaluation will not improve the overall quality of the university system.

After two years of discussion, the national *Consejo de Universidades* approved, in September 1992, an "experimental programme of evaluation of the quality of the university system" by institutional evaluation. The process, started in early 1993 and completed in 1994, was based initially on self-assessment as a method of stimulating self-reflection in the units to be evaluated, offering them the opportunity to ask themselves questions about their teaching programmes, their research and their services. Each university formed an evaluation committee which collected information from within the university itself, from the students, the staff and the academics and administrators. The self-evaluation produced by the evaluation committee was assessed by an external committee appointed by the national *Consejo de Universidades* which included experts from the areas under evaluation. The external committee revised the self-evaluation, by visiting the institution and interviewing the people involved (teachers, non-teaching staff, managers and students). This trial programme was judged to be successful and formed the basis for the National Programme for University Evaluation (*Plan Nacional de Evaluación de la Calidad de las Universidades*) launched in 1996.

Quality control is now based on a precise and complex model, based on successful systems in other countries, such as the Netherlands, suggested by OECD (1986). For the evaluation of teaching, the input (student qualifications and teaching staff selection and status), as well as the process (quantity and quality of teaching, methodology, type of assessment, etc.) are taken into consideration, with particular attention paid to the context (infrastructure, resources, socio-economical environment). For the evaluation of research, the Spanish model takes into consideration some of the most common criteria, such as scientific production (with preference for international publications) and participation in research programmes; but other more specific indicators come from the analysis of the resources available and of departmental life. Finally, the evaluation of management is based both on a cost-benefit analysis and on the efficiency of the institution in improving the quality of teaching and research. However, another important criteria is the view of the institution by users for which feed-back from students, teaching and non teaching staff, the public administration, and the local and regional community is taken into account.

Economy, society and new perspectives

The "university explosion" took place in Spain later than in other European countries and in rather difficult circumstances. It happened more as a consequence of democratic reconstruction and political reorganisation, than in response to the needs of a flourishing and expanding economy. It started during the international recession within a still fragile economy, it accompanied the transition to a democratic political system and it seems not to have taken account of the crisis of confidence in the economic and social impact of education originating in Europe and the United States. It is because of this that Spanish social policy has continued to emphasise the role of education, in particular at secondary and university level, while in many countries, restrictions of various kinds are being put on educational expansion. This has had some negative consequences as Spanish citizens have opted for the expanded degree and career offerings without worrying about the possible consequences.

This has led to a rather contradictory situation. In a country where the unemployment rate is higher than the European average, and does not seem to be decreasing despite the massive economic growth which followed the entrance of Spain into the European Union, the proportion of unemployed qualified young people, many with university degrees, is higher than the proportion of unqualified young people. This is a consequence of a governmental policy, often criticised by the unions, that aimed to offer young people, regardless of their qualification, a variety of "deregulated" job opportunities, from which university graduates have profited less than other social groups.

However, the picture is not the same for all fields of study nor for the entire job market: public services, in particular health and education, as well as professions involving technicians and scientists, are areas of the job market where considerable growth has taken place over the last 15 years and public services were, and still are the largest source of employment for university graduates. This is a characteristic feature of the relationship between higher education and the economy in southern European and less industrialised countries. Spain can however be considered to be one of the European Union member states which is most rapidly abandoning this traditional feature. Universities are at the cross-roads of this development. While the corporate interests of part of the academic staff and management are resistant to the adjustment of higher education to social and labour demands, there are already many examples of the development of links and co-operation between higher education, industry, service companies and social organisations and of formal agreements for joint scientific and professional collaboration. Last, but not least, the process of europeanisation and internationalisation of Spanish higher education and society seems to be reconstructing new links between present and past Spanish culture in Europe and across the Atlantic.

United States

The system of higher education in the United States is large and diverse and as a result, extreme caution should be exercised before presenting brush-stroke accounts. However, a number of themes can be discussed to highlight the uniqueness of the system. Firstly, it is far larger than other national systems with over 14 million students and 800 000 staff spread over around 3 600 institutions. Nearly half of the students were enrolled on a part-time basis and over 80% were over 25 years of age.

Secondly, a characteristic of educational provision in the United States is that it is highly devolved and decentralised to the level of the state. Each state system has developed its own characteristics and it is difficult to talk about "national" trends within American higher education. As a result, there are no centralised mediating agencies between the federal government and state educational systems in the United States. However, buffer agencies were created to guide the relationship between the state and higher educational institutions which performed functions such as defining missions, reviewing programmes and budgets, developing state-wide information systems and in many cases, establishing the numbers and distribution of students.

Thirdly, higher education in the United States is multi-layered and multi-sectoral. The primary division within the system exists between public and private institutions. The scale of private institutions, numbering 1 800, is unique throughout the world and only a few other systems, such as Japan and Brazil, have private institutions on this scale. However, the boundaries between public and private sectors are blurring as public universities receive money from private sources such as alumni, and private universities seek federal and state support. These public and private institutions co-exist with a third layer comprised of a well-developed network of local community colleges.

There is an element of division of labour between these institutions in that activities at the community colleges are largely demand-driven and adapt to the short and medium term needs of the local labour market, the state universities deal with longer range and more strategic needs of an educated and skilled workforce and the private universities are involved heavily in research and doctoral education. Apart from these three main types, there are other institutional forms such as doctoral- and research-based universities, comprehensive universities, liberal arts colleges, specialised institutions and those dedicated to certain groups such as women or religious and ethnic groups.

Further, the system is heavily market-led with much competition for students, staff and resources. Competition between states is one of the defining elements of the American higher education system, in which each state aids its HE system to compete for national funds. As a result, the system is characterised by a high level of initiative and entrepreneurialism which brings together public and private partners to increase the competitiveness of institutions. To a much greater extent than other national systems, this includes drawing upon alumni support. Such support has increased the diversity of funding streams to higher education institutions which, in turn, has increased their autonomy. This applies equally to private and public institutions.

In spite of this overriding emphasis on competition, there is also co-ordination within the system. In the absence of nationally co-ordinating bodies, the system is characterised by high levels of "voluntary association" which creates linkages between the highly decentralised and autonomous parts of the system. Further, state master plans guide significant proportions of the student market towards certain institutions. In particular, the significant differences between in-state and out-of-state tuition fees encourage most students to study at one of their local state institutions. However, the brighter and wealthier students have the additional advantage of being able to choose the best public or even private institutions, both in or out of state.

One may expect, then, that considering the significant level of decentralisation and state responsibility shown by many higher education institutions in the United States, meeting regional needs would be a strong characteristic of the national system. Both the community colleges and the public universities are heavily involved in local and regional economic development in the United States. Legal authority for public colleges and universities are vested in boards which are comprised of business people, professionals and civic leaders, and not university members, who are appointed or elected by the state. In this context, boards have the interests of the university and the state in mind. In most states, systems have been established to co-ordinate the numerous public institutions to avoid duplication and competition for resources.

The most striking contribution of the American higher education system to meeting regional needs comes from the Land Grant institutions. The original constitution of the United States in 1787 promoted higher education through the North-West Ordnance which prompted the sale of public land for the support of education. This was the forerunner of the land grant tradition in the United States – the granting of federal land for the sole use of higher education. The official granting of land to establish a Land Grant university in every state was achieved through the Morrill (Land Grant) Act of 1862. The Land Grant universities were seen as the "people's universities" which were based upon the idea of educational opportunity and service to the public. Since their inception, then, such institutions have an embedded commitment to serve the state.

The Land Grant institutions were particularly focused upon providing practical information on subjects connected with agriculture and as a result play a central role in the development of the agricultural industry in the United States. They also play a key role in the democratisation of higher education in the United States, seen most recently by the incorporation of 29 Native American colleges into the Land Grant system in 1994 to establish agricultural extension programmes focused upon the needs of native Americans. Today, the National Association of State Universities and Land Grant Colleges (NASULGC) has member campuses in all 50 states in the United States.

The Land Grant universities gain their distinctiveness by combining the pure intellect of the German Humboldtian tradition and the raw pragmatism of American populism. Hence, their focus became the application of learning to service. This unique historical development has contributed to the legacy of public service and volunteering within Land Grant universities. NASULGC has sought the support of the W.K. Kellogg Foundation to investigate the future of state and Land Grant universities. As a result of this partnership, the Kellogg Commission was established and involves 24 partner universities and an advisory council of community leaders to create an agenda for change and promote best practice in five areas: the student experience, access, engaged institutions, a learning society, and campus culture. The third of these, "engaged institutions" is seeking ways in which universities can go beyond "outreach" to become more engaged with the societies it serves through the mutual development of goals and the two-way sharing of ideas. It is clear then, that debates relating to the issue of university-regional relationships are extremely pertinent to a system such as that found in the United States which, to a large extent, is devolved and state-led, and has a notion of community service and engagement enshrined within its public institutions.

However, more than many other national systems, the HE system in the United States represents an experimentation with non-placed, virtual and corporate-led educational provision. This can be seen through organisations such as Motorola University, the University of Phoenix and the Western Governors University which highlight the ability to transcend the traditional model of the university and provide tailor-made courses to groups across large parts of the world.

Bibliography

AMIN, A. and THRIFT, N.J. (1994),
Globalisation, Institutions and Regional Development in Europe, Oxford University Press.

CLARK, B.R. (1998),
Creating Entrepreneurial Universities: Organizational Pathways of Transformation, Pergamon, Oxford.

CURDS (1997),
"The Northern Region in the Information Society: An Outline Benchmarking Study and SWOT Analysis – Draft Report".

DAHLLÖF, U. *et al.* (1998),
Towards the Responsive University: The Regional Role of Eastern Finland Universities, Finnish Higher Education Evaluation Council, Helsinki.

DAVIES, J.L. (1997),
"The Regional University: Issues in the Development of an Organisational Framework", *Higher Education Management*, Vol. 9, No. 3, OECD, Paris, pp. 29-42.

DAVIES, J.L. (1998),
The Public Role of the University: The Dialogue of Universities with their Stakeholders: Comparisons Between Different Regions of Europe, CRE.

DEETYA (1998),
"Learning for Life – Final Report", *Review of Higher Education Financing and Policy*, Canberra, Australia.

DETR (1997),
Building Partnerships for Prosperity: Sustainable Growth, Competitiveness and Employment in the English Regions, Cm 3814, TSO, London.

DfEE (1998*a*),
Universities and Economic Development, Higher Education and Employment Division, TSO, London.

DfEE (1998*b*),
The Learning Age: A Renaissance for a New Britain, Green Paper, Cm 3790, TSO, London.

DTI (1998),
Our Competitive Future: Building the Knowledge Driven Economy, TSO, London.

DUKE, C. (1998),
"Lifelong Learning: Implications for the University of the 21st Century", *Higher Education Management*, Vol. 11, No. 1, OECD, Paris, pp. 19-36.

FLORIDA, R. (1995),
"Toward the Learning Region", *Futures*, 27 (5), pp. 527-536.

GARLICK, S. (1998),
Creative Associations in Special Places: Enhancing the Partnership Role of Universities in Building Competitive Regional Economies, Southern Cross Regional Research Institute, Southern Cross University, Australia.

de GAUDEMAR, J-P. (1997),
"The Higher Education Institution as a Regional Actor", *Higher Education Management*, Vol. 9, No. 2, OECD, Paris, pp. 53-64.

GIBBONS, M., LIMOGES, C., NOWOTNY, H., SCHWARTZWAN, S., TROW, M. and SCOTT, P. (1994),
The New Production of Knowledge: The Dynamics of Science and Research in Contemporary Societies, Sage, London.

GODDARD, J.B. (1998),
"Managing the University/Regional Interface", *Higher Education Management*, Vol. 9, No. 3, OECD, Paris, pp. 7-28.

GODDARD, J.B. and CHATTERTON, P. (1999),
« Regional Development Agencies and the Knowledge Economy: Harnessing the Potential of Universities », *Environment and Planning – Government and Policy*.

GODDARD, J.B., CHARLES, D., PIKE, A., POTTS, G. and BRADLEY, D. (1994),
Universities and Communities, CVCP, London.

HÖLTTÄ, S. and PULLIAINEN, K. (1996),
"The Changing Regional Role of Universities", *Tertiary Education and Management*, Vol. 2, No. 2.

HOWELLS, J., NEDEVA, M. and GEORGHIOU, L. with the assistance from J. Evans and S. Hinder (1998),
Industry-academic Links in the United Kingdom, PREST, University of Manchester.

KANTER, R.M. (1995),
World Class: Thriving Locally in the Global Economy, Simon and Schuster, New York.

KELLOGG COMMISSION (1997),
Returning to our Roots: The Student Experience, National Association of State Universities and Land-Grant Colleges, Washington.

LUNDVALL, B.-Å. (1992),
National Systems of Innovation. Towards a Theory of Innovation and Interactive Learning, Pinter, London.

LUNDVALL, B.-Å. and JOHNSON, B. (1994),
"The Learning Economy", *Journal of Industry Studies*, No. 2, pp. 23-42.

MCNICOLL, I.H., MCCLUSKY, K. and KELLY, U. (1997),
The Impact of Universities and Colleges on the United Kingdom Economy, CVCP, London.

NATIONAL COMMITTEE OF INQUIRY INTO HIGHER EDUCATION (1997),
Chapter 12: The Local and Regional Role of Higher Education, TSO, London.

OECD (1986),
Reviews of National Policies for Education: Spain, Paris.

OECD (1996),
Reviews of National Policies for Education: France, Paris.

PUTNAM, R.D, LEONARDI, R. and NANETTI, R.Y. (1993),
   Making Democracy Work: Civic Traditions in Modern Italy, Princetown University
   Press, Princetown.

ROBSON, B., DRAKE, K. and IAIN, D. (1997),
   Higher Education and Regions, Report 9, The National Committee of Inquiry into
   Higher Education, HMSO, London.

SCOTT, P. (1995),
   The Meanings of Mass Higher Education, SRHE, Buckingham.

STORPER, M. (1995),
   "The Resurgence of Regional Economies, Ten Years Later: The Region as a
   Nexus of Untraded Interdependencies", *European Urban and Regional Studies*,
   Vol. 2 (3), pp. 191-221.

UNESCO (1998),
   Framework for Priority Action for Change and Development of Higher Education, Paris.

OECD PUBLICATIONS, 2, rue André-Pascal, 75775 PARIS CEDEX 16
PRINTED IN FRANCE
(89 1999 11 1 P) ISBN 92-64-17143-6 – No. 50983 1999